Every woman will discover in *Woman Meets Jesus* the freedom to overcome bondage to religion and to live an honest, grace-filled faith.
—LIS VAN HARTEN, Director of Sustaining Pastoral and Congregational Excellence, Christian Reformed Church of North America, Grand Rapids, MI

This book is perfect for church groups to read and discuss, using the questions following each chapter's wonderfully described encounters between Jesus and women.
—PHYLLIS BALZER PALS, Adult Education Committee Chair, Plymouth Congregational Church, Coconut Grove, FL

The book captures God's bountiful love for us and leads us to experience a lavishly grateful spirit in our own lives.
—KATHY KLOMPEEN, Executive Assistant to the President, Bastyr University, Bothell, WA

Deeply touched by the emotions that surfaced while reading these compelling stories, I realized that Jesus has a very special relationship with me and all women.
—MYRIAM ZAYAS, RN, BSN, Miller School of Medicine, University of Miami, Department of Pediatric Hematology-Oncology

Woman Meets Jesus takes my breath away. Jesus' compassion for women is as stunning today as it must have been 2,000 years ago.
—QUENTIN J. SCHULTZE, author of *Communicating for Life* and *Here I Am*

This book is for all who have struggled with being close to Jesus—and who wonder where they fit in as a Christian mother, daughter, or sister. It gave me the courage to open the door to my heart so Jesus will continue to help me grow.
—SHARON MOLENDYK, Bible study leader, Miami Florida

Each chapter is an eye-opening experience which helps me reflect on my life with a new set of spectacles custom fitted to my life as female.
—ELSA GARCIA, elementary school educator

Woman Meets Jesus showed my book group how Jesus' love and compassion transformed the lives of women who were often rejected, abused, misunderstood, sick, and feeling worthless.
—CHRISTINE BAIRD, Miami, Florida

I now realize the healing work of Jesus in my life is an ongoing process, not just a one-time dying for my sins, but a day-by-day healing of what drags me down.
—MARINA HAKKERS, Miami, Florida

Reading this book led me personally to recognize, accept, and live God's promises—just like the women Jesus interacted with 2,000 years ago.
—ERIKA VOERMAN, California and the Netherlands

This is a deeply inspiring, woman-to-woman memoir, written from the heart with knowledge and wisdom for us to share with our family and friends.
—HELENA PEREZ, Miami, Florida and Columbia

Woman Meets Jesus enlists historical imagination and spiritual insight to create portraits of Jesus' encounters with women that powerfully affirm the living Christ who makes all hearts restless until they rest in him.
—DANIEL L. PALS, Professor of Religious Studies and History, University of Miami

WOMAN
meets
JESUS

WOMAN

meets

JESUS

*How Jesus Encourages, Empowers, and Equips
Women on Their Personal Journey of Faith*

Ruth Vander Zee

foreword by
Mary Albert Darling

preface by
Caryn Dahlstrand Rivadeneira

edenridge press
GRAND RAPIDS, MICHIGAN

Published by
Edenridge Press LLC
Grand Rapids, Michigan USA
www.edenridgepress.com
service@edenridgepress.com

Quantity discount pricing is available.
service@edenridgepress.com
Fax: (616) 365-5797

Design and illustration by Matthew Plescher
Edited by Quentin J. Schultze and Amy Tol

Vander Zee, Ruth
    Woman meets Jesus: how Jesus encourages, empowers, and equips women on their personal faith journeys / Ruth Vander Zee ; foreword by Mary A. Darling ; preface by Caryn Dahlstrand Rivadeneira

ISBN 9780982706350 (alk. Paper)
Library of Congress Control Number: 2011930804

REL012130   RELIGION / Christian Life / Women's Issues

Printed in the United States of America

v-3

Dedicated to my sister Jan—a woman who has met Jesus

Acknowledgments

Special thanks to Chris Baird, Sharon Molendyk, Renee Mandel, Vanda Fromvald, Alicia Heinrich, Gladys Nelson, Flory White, Marina Hakkers, Maggie Dokic, Vera McKenzie, Andrea Baena, Sonya Diaz, Tena Admiraal, Louise Oliver, Erika Voerman, Diane Averill, Pete Mans, Don Ridder, Carol Beezhold, Ray and Wilma Gunnink, Peter Broers, Jan Ornee, Marianne Tigchelaar, Helena Perez, Myriam Zayas, Phyllis Pals, and Dan Pals who not only read the manuscript to see where I touched the heart but also helped me see where I missed the mark so I could edit.

Thanks as well to Quentin Schultze and Matt Plescher, who paid attention to details and produced a beautiful book—because beautiful books are wonderful to hold in your hand.

And to my husband and best friend, Vern, who not only loves me but believed in this project and tirelessly fact-checked, inspired, and encouraged me to keep going.

A Personal Note from Ruth

Dear Companion:

Thanks so much for joining me on a journey with Jesus and many women like us that he loves so deeply. I'm honored.

May I encourage you to read *Woman Meets Jesus* in a way that will nurture your walk with our Lord of grace?

While writing the book, I imagined it being used:

- ∾ As a *personal study*, with a cup of coffee or tea and a journal beside you. Read the lesson and allow the Holy Spirit to lead as you answer the questions.
- ∾ As a *group study*, with women reading the chapter before they come and a leader guiding the group through the questions at the end of each chapter.
- ∾ As a *group study*, with one person assigned to "be" the woman in the chapter. She could read or use her acting skills—presenting the first-person account as a soliloquy while the leader guides the questions and conversation of the chapter.

Please visit my website for more ideas and to send me an email about your experiences with *Woman Meets Jesus*. You may also invite me to lead a seminar on the book at your church or even for a group of congregations in your area.

May our Lord encourage, empower, and equip you on your journey of faith!

Gratefully,
Ruth

www.journey-of-faith.com

Contents

xi

Foreword

Woman Meets Jesus compassionately explores the hunger that we all feel to be known, accepted, and loved for who we really are—not for how others see and judge us. The women Jesus encountered were truly hungry for such intimate love. So are women today. So are men. This is a deeply human hunger that is so hard for us all to satisfy.

Some days it seems impossible. Alongside this hunger are our temptations to hide particular thoughts, feelings, and actions—especially self-destructive ones. We hope that if others don't see the hidden parts of us, maybe then they'll love and accept us. But we also know that the more we hide our hearts from others the less they will know us as we really are. How can others possibly love us if they don't actually know us intimately? How can we love others if we don't truly know them intimately?

When we're honest with ourselves, we recognize that living without integrity—with a gap between who we are inside and who we pretend to be to others—is a lie. We become walking, talking deceivers. Today we might say that we are inauthentic persons in relationships with other inauthentic persons. Sometimes a bit of self-honesty is enough for us to truly begin living a more integrated and authentic life.

But even when we realize our disordered ways of living, we're still plagued by fear, anxiety, insecurity, jealousy, and low self-esteem. If we don't feel such things we're probably suffering from an inflated ego; we think more highly of ourselves than we should. What we don't always realize is the depth of our bondage to our false selves—of the stubborn bondage that distorts our relationships with God, others, and ourselves.

Those of us who admit that we suffer from such inauthentic living know how hard it is to rid ourselves of bad habits and destructive thoughts, including our tendency to hide from others and God. The apostle Paul told the church in Rome, "For I have the desire to do what is good, but I cannot carry it out. For what I do is not the good I want to do; no, the evil I do not want to do—this I keep on doing" (7:18b–19). Paul didn't tell the Romans exactly what it was that so troubled him about himself. Even as the first great theologian of the Christian faith, he suffered from his legendary but undefined "thorn in the flesh" (2 Cor. 12:7–10).

But Paul also proclaimed, "It is for freedom that Christ has set us free" (Gal. 5:1).

Freedom. Isn't that what we all hunger for? Like the Bible says, we can be set free from whatever binds us, whether a long-standing hurt or habit we can't seem to let go of, or an obsession or addiction that we aren't sure we can live without—and maybe don't want to lay aside because it is such a significant part of our self-identity.

The good news is that Jesus came to show us how to live in freedom instead of bondage. Jesus' own encounters with women addressed their bondages with the offer of true, life-changing liberty. Jesus offered them the kind of freedom that remakes a

person from the heart outward, not the kind that merely adds
to the contemporary cultural facades. We can read about this
freedom throughout the Bible, but it takes special forms when
Jesus interacts with women. He cares personally about their own,
individual bondage.

But can we experience such freedom ourselves—personally?
Can we accept it? Own it? Live it? Do we women, in particular,
have the courage to honestly confront our hunger?

The Bible is not meant only to be read. At the heart of the
Bible is a person. Scripture is meant to be experienced relation-
ally as the living Word—as the Word made flesh. That's why I'm
deeply excited about Ruth Vander Zee's book. Ruth understands
the Bible as the living Word, as an encounter with the very living
God. She also understands what can keep us from authentic living
and *what*—better yet, *who*—can free us from ourselves.

Ruth takes us through powerful stories of real women who
encountered Jesus while he walked the earth, and who, through
their encounters with the rabbi, found freedom, peace, and joy. By
putting herself in these women's shoes, Ruth makes Jesus' interactions with them come alive in ways that relate to Ruth's story and
to our own personal life journeys. Ruth personalizes the stories
of women who, like us, have the opportunity to personally meet
their greatest living advocate.

You'll be surprised at how much you identify with the
thoughts and feelings of the women who lived two millennia ago
in a very different part of the world. No matter what you may be
dealing with in your life—such as fear, insecurity, insignificance,
lack of acceptance, approval-seeking, burnout, fatigue, or even
misguided good intentions—you'll find women in these pages
who dealt with the same issues. You'll also discover hope and
healing in their stories. By placing yourself in these women's shoes,
you'll encounter the radical Jesus who encouraged, empowered,

and equipped women in life-changing ways. Through Ruth's powerful retelling of these stories you'll find the freedom they found—the freedom that transforms your relationships and helps renew the world—all for the glory of God.

—MARY ALBERT DARLING
Co-author with Tony Campolo of *The God of Intimacy and Action* (2007) and *Connecting Like Jesus* (2010), and Associate Professor of Communication and Spiritual Formation, Spring Arbor University

Preface

In *Are Women Human?*, Dorothy Sayers writes,

Perhaps it is no wonder that women were the first at the Cradle
and the last at the Cross. They had never known a man like this
Man—there never has been another. A prophet and teacher
who never nagged at them, never flattered or coaxed or patron-
ized; who never made arch jokes about them, never treated
them as 'The women, God help us!' or 'The ladies, God bless
them!'; who rebuked without querulousness and praised without condescension; who took their arguments seriously; who
never mapped out their sphere for them, never urged them to
be feminine or jeered at them for being female; who had no
axe to grind and no uneasy male dignity to defend; who took
them as he found them and was completely unself-conscious.
There is no act, no sermon, no parable in the whole Gospel that
borrows its pungency from female perversity; nobody could
possibly guess from the words or deeds of Jesus that there was
anything 'funny' about woman's nature" (46–47).

Having read Ruth Vander Zee's splendid book on Jesus' encounters with women, I know that she shares Sayers' passion for Christ. I do, too—even more now that Ruth's passionate telling of the encounters has revived my faith in the radical rabbi. This book will cut to your heart, too. You'll confront Jesus on his journey to minister to women in a society that had little time and space for females.

I confess: while the story of Jesus and the woman at the well should impress me for its great theological truths and historic moments, instead my knees go weak. While I should remember to focus on the things that really matter, when I read Jesus praising Mary for learning at his feet, my heart beats faster. When the bleeding woman touches Jesus' cloak and he turns—without shuddering at her contaminating touch—and tells the woman, "Your faith has healed you," I should celebrate her faith and Jesus' healing power, but instead I make the sign of the cross and put a hand to my heart. And while the story of the resurrected Jesus first appearing to Mary Magdalene should make me rejoice in our risen Lord, every time I get to the part where Jesus gently says, "Mary," I swoon.

Please don't get me wrong. I don't have a *crush* on Jesus. I just love him—deeply, dearly. And while I love him most for the grace he offers and the life he lived—and gave—I'm not ashamed to say I love him for the way he was with women.

If you've ever felt ostracized or excluded, ignored or belittled, if your gifts have been passed over because of what the Bible "clearly says" about the roles of women, then you likely understand. Because while we may argue about just how clear the Bible really is about those roles, Jesus' view of women is far more spacious.

Jesus seemed to have slight concern for the "rules" and "roles" for women. After all, women were among the lost he came to seek and save. So, in a world where women had no voice, no power, Jesus listened to women and empowered them. Where women were shunned, Jesus reached out to them personally.

Where women were uneducated, Jesus taught them wisely. Where women were dismissed as unreliable sources, Jesus entrusted women to bear witness to the most important news ever—first, proclaiming his status as the Messiah and then announcing his resurrection.

In fact, when I was younger—struggling with a Christian tradition that seemed to devalue me and my gifts because I was a woman—Ruth was one of the "older" (sorry, Ruth!) women in my life who first helped me understand that the way Jesus talked to, respected, and loved women looked very different than what I witnessed even in the church. This understanding, this realization that Jesus didn't devalue me, helped save—and shape—my faith. Ruth was Christ's compassionate love to me precisely because she had been smitten by the rabbi's love for her.

Because of this, I came to Ruth's book expecting to love it before I read the first word—and her book didn't disappoint. In fact, in these pages, she goes far beyond what I had hoped for by taking every reader deeper into the stories of these women. Instead of simply reiterating the implications of Jesus' interactions with women for us today, Ruth has us settle back and focus on what it meant for *them*. Using her background and talents as a storyteller, Ruth drops us right into these stories, allowing us to see what these women observed, feel what they felt, to help us experience what these women would have thought and felt and to experience just how Jesus changed their lives. In examining and re-telling their personal stories, Ruth not only invites us to enter into their lives but to enter our own stories into God's story. She invites us to focus and reflect on how the love and presence of Jesus in the world over two thousand years ago—and his presence today—have changed our lives as women. She asks us to recall the moment we first encountered Jesus—and all the moments that have followed. If we've never really encountered the radical rabbi, she invites us to meet him along the road of our journeys of faith and doubt.

Of course, any discussion along these lines might elicit accusations of putting "feminism" above faith. But this is misguided. Exploring the way Jesus interacted with women isn't about feminism or proving any ideological point. Instead, it's about Jesus. It's about getting to know him—through the stories of these women he loved, empowered, liberated, taught, healed, and forgave.

After all, as Ruth writes, "We are women who have met Jesus because Jesus went out of his way to meet us."

So read on, and be moved by Ruth's beautiful book as much as I was. Enter into the stories. Add your own. And most importantly, get to know and love the Jesus who went out of his way to meet us and to get to know us more intimately.

—CARYN DAHLSTRAND RIVADENEIRA
Contributes regularly to *Christianity Today's*
Her.Meneutics blog. Her books include *Grumble Hallelujah: Learning to Love Your Life Even When It Lets You Down* and *Mama's Got a Fake ID.*

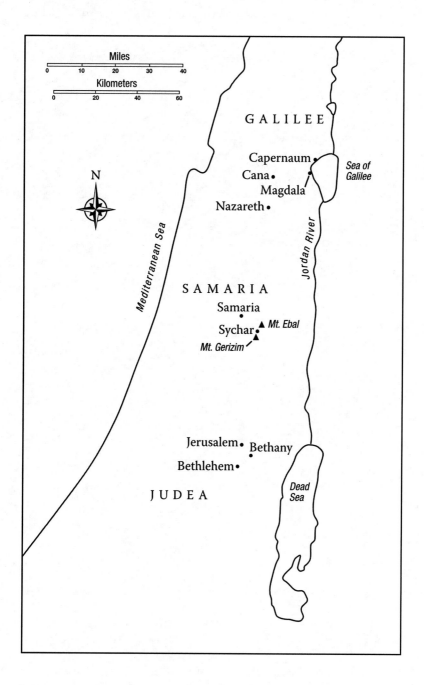

There once was a man, his name John, sent by God to point out the way to the LIFE-LIGHT. He came to show everyone where to look, who to believe in. John was not himself the Light; he was there to show the way to the Light.

The LIFE-LIGHT [Jesus] was the real thing:
> *Every person entering LIFE he brings into the LIGHT.*
He was in the world,
> *the world was there through him,*
>> *and yet the world didn't even notice.*
He came to his own people, but they didn't want him.
>> *But whoever did want him,*
>> *who believed he was who he claimed*
>> *and would do what he said,*
>> *HE MADE TO BE THEIR TRUE SELVES,*
>> *their child-of-God selves.*
> *These are the God-begotten, not blood-begotten, not flesh-begotten, not sex-begotten.*

The Word became flesh and blood, and moved into the neighborhood.
We saw the glory with our own eyes,
The one-of-a-kind glory,
Like Father, like Son,
Generous inside and out,
True from start to finish.

John 1 (*The Message*, capitals added)

Introduction

Several years ago, I wakened to hollow drumming. I recognized the sound of round, plastic garbage containers rolling down the street, calunking handles interrupting their drunken morning stroll across lawns and down my street. In my morning haze, I felt sorry for the poor neighbor whose garbage was sure to be playing tag outside on the blustery spring morning. But when I lifted the blinds to reassure myself that my garbage container was still standing sentinel in front of my house, I saw no garbage container.

Wrapping a robe around my still bed-warm body, I ran down the stairs and opened the front door. Looking down the street and seeing no sign of my runaway, I followed the direction of the wind to the water retention pond at the end of the street. There I found my garbage can, playfully bouncing on the edge of the pond. Empty.

All the garbage of my week was now a ring of refuse around that retention pond. Everything I had discarded was on display. And what was worse, I couldn't just haul my garbage can home and pretend that all the debris wasn't mine. My name and address were on all the envelopes—everything from junk mail, political fliers, and investment company envelopes to important and unimportant letters and documents. Snotty tissues from my persistent cold, grapefruit rinds, bread wrappers, crushed cereal boxes, and the two containers of Ben and Jerry's Chunky Monkey I ate during last week's ice cream binge. It was all there. The litter of my life was now littering this pond, and anyone with any curiosity could see the refuse of my week and assess my discards.

I felt exposed. Somehow, I thought my garbage was private. I didn't think my neighbors—who had their own garbage—should be able to stand on the edge of the pond and peruse mine.

But, as usual, I was in a hurry. And I had to make a hurried decision. I knew I could go home, get a rake, and spend several hours cleaning up this mess. But I didn't have time. I had to get going for an early-morning meeting at school. I took my chances and hoped that everybody else was also busy—so busy they wouldn't have time to go to the pond. So I dragged my garbage can home, went to school, attended my meetings, and taught my classes, thinking all day about the mess I had left behind and the miserable job of cleaning it up I would face when I got home.

That evening, I turned the corner into my neighborhood and—with a feeling of dread about what I would see—glanced towards the retention pond. I saw clear, rippling water. The lowering sun was painting beautiful pictures on this now-pristine little body of water. My mess was gone; every shred of my morning debris had been cleaned up. It had all been carried away. Someone had come during the day and removed every trace of my garbage. They obviously knew where to find me; my address was on every envelope. But no one ever left a bill for the cleanup.

I have thought often about that morning. Standing on the edge of the pond, I had wondered if the mess before me was a picture of confession. I could no longer hope the soggy debris came from somebody else's garbage can. It was mine and anyone who chose to look could see it. Yet my public dumping was cleaned up by some unknown person who never scolded or demanded payment for services rendered! For me, this was a life-altering experience.

If I had my druthers, I'd cover the refuse of my life with a lid. Frankly, I prefer to keep my private sins and my private hurts to myself. Lord knows I have plenty of public ones. But that's exactly where grace breaks in. It's the only place for grace to become evident—in the middle of messes. In the decay.

Jesus sees my heart's decay clearly. And I know he is the one who can clean me up and will never scold or demand payment for services rendered. Not only that, he welcomes me to walk along beside him, day by day, as he processes and heals and equips me to live, as he said so often, "in peace." That is life-altering!

But the funny thing about garbage is that it decomposes a little more each day in the heat of life. Our olfactory nerves tire easily and we don't recognize the smell. We don't notice the beginning of decay.

In the same way, we don't recognize the decay in our hearts. The decay that does not give life. The decay that hides in the darkness of our spirit. The decay that resists the refining work of the Holy Spirit and keeps us from living generously with ourselves or with others. The decay that keeps us hiding parts of our heart underneath some kind of bushel.

Hiding comes rather naturally. It is a knee-jerk response when we feel badly about something we've done or said. At least, if I'm being honest, that's what I do. I can stuff garbage into the bottom of the can and cover it up with something less noxious with the best of them. But stuffing isn't healthy. Living dishonestly before God and others does not help us flourish.

Adding to that, we come up with long lists of what we think makes God happy and what makes us look good in the eyes of others. We feel secure when we know what's on the okay and not-okay lists because then we don't have to figure out how our hidden parts are influencing everything that comes our way. All of these lists keep us busy and we don't have the time or energy to deal with, really deal with, the hidden hurts buried deep within. There may be very good items on our lists. They may include going the extra mile. Feeding the homeless. Standing up for the disenfranchised. Helping natural-disaster victims overseas. Not lusting. Being perfect as our heavenly Father is perfect. Who can say anything bad about any of these things? Our lists help us define what we do and what we don't do—our "shoulds" and "should nots"—how we should act, with whom we should associate, which political issues God would support, and which bandwagon he would be on. The rules we follow help us know the *right* way to do things and are instructive on how to be a holy person. We know God's desires because our lists tell us.

But lists do not satisfy. The good things on my lists didn't heal the decaying stuff hidden deep within. My lists didn't satisfy the hunger within me for a relationship with Jesus. In fact, I had heard that "relationship with Jesus" phrase so often that it had lost its meaning.

That one morning, when my garbage can decided to run away, initiated the beginning of a journey for me. The God who knew the way I think and the way I process information sent me a very personal metaphor. One I couldn't escape. Straight down from heaven above. A picture of grace right in front of my own house.

And in every "pond experience" Jesus comes and says, "I'm here to clean up. Free of charge. Each one of your messes—one at a time. If you bring them up to the light, we can do this together. Trust me. I can do it. You can be free. You can have peace." He invites us to live in his presence. To live as if he lives in the house with us. As if we walk and talk together. As if he sits in the recliner watching TV with us. As if he chops onions next to us when we're preparing dinner. As if he stirs the paint when we're redecorating the kids' bedroom.

Why? Because more than he likes us, he loves us. He cares about us, lists or not. Because he knows that for us to be healthy and whole we need to trust that in his presence there is healing for not only our deepest wounds, but for the scratches and bruises we acquire along the way as well.

And when we're in the presence of the grace-giving Jesus who loves us to the core, something amazing happens to us. Grace breaks in. Grace is like that. Slowly. Day by day. Little by little. Through the power of his presence and the light of his love, we can be healed. We can make progress in forgiving the ones who hurt us. Forgiveness comes off the to-do list and becomes more of a natural, life-giving response. We can be more generous. More faithful. More honoring to others. Anger, lust, and coveting no longer grip us tightly. We can speak the truth caringly. We can concentrate on the positive. We can decide that if something has a solution, we don't have to worry about it. And if it doesn't have a solution, we don't have to worry.

When we live with Jesus, we can feel complete. We can feel like we are not lonely because the one who loves us most is right there with us. We can silence the negative, destructive voices we have heard for a lifetime. We can decide to eat what is healthy instead of eating compulsively. We can look in the mirror and see a beautiful woman looking back at us. We can see our youth as the beginning of wisdom and our wrinkles as life lessons learned. We can put away exasperation and find patience. We can have a peace that doesn't come from somewhere outside of ourselves but from within. We can deal with our issues, not by clouding them with pills or alcohol or other self-abuse, but by inviting Jesus to be with us.

And we can do all these things, not because they are on a to-do or not-to-do list, but because they become natural responses. They are the effects of living in the healing presence of Jesus. That's what Jesus' grace does: it can transform us at our core.

My loving heavenly Father nudged me into slowing down and beginning a quest to scratch the surface of Jesus' grace. Jesus taught, healed, and ministered out of a heart of grace. That's why he was such a radical rabbi. I wanted to see that grace, which he liberally offered to everyone.

But, as a woman, I was especially curious. What was it like to be a woman in the crowd surrounding Jesus? Did women come to Jesus with the same issues as men? Did Jesus relate differently to men than to women? I wanted to know how he related to the needs of women. I wanted to meet those women who had become part of the fabric of his life. Those he healed. Those he empowered. Those to whom he was kind. Those with whom he conversed. Those with whom he broke cultural norms. I wanted to see Jesus through the heart of a woman.

Always, right below the surface, just past the obvious, I made discoveries. I discovered women who trusted Jesus, challenged him, loved him, questioned him, and believed him.

And as they interacted with Jesus, I found myself in the middle of their stories. I saw Jesus care about the stuff that lay hidden in their hearts. These women met Jesus before he suffered and died for their sins. Before he was buried, descended to hell, and rose again. They met Jesus who cared about their heart's deepest needs. He not only cared about their obvious issues—the issues everybody saw and knew about—but about the layers underneath that had probably bothered them since third grade. The layers of stuff they didn't even think were important. Things they dismissed as inconsequential, but which actually colored their decisions, attitudes, actions—every part of their lives. When these women trusted Jesus, he gave them hope and healing. Faith and freedom. Grace and glory. And time after time, their stories intersected with mine. I was interacting with Jesus, too.

Some years after my glimpse of Jesus on a blustery spring morning, my daughter fell from a ladder into dirt and mulch in her front yard. She didn't fall very far, but the damage to her right

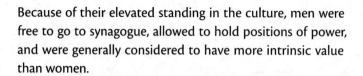

Because of their elevated standing in the culture, men were free to go to synagogue, allowed to hold positions of power, and were generally considered to have more intrinsic value than women.

Imagine a woman who

-  because of what she had been taught, considered herself to be inherently inferior to all men.
- had been told since she was small that she was physically inferior because of her natural bodily functions, which made her unclean before God.
- was considered first the property of her father and later the property of her husband.
- had little or no authority just because of her gender.
- could not testify in court because she was not considered a credible witness.

Imagine her surprise when she met Jesus, who spoke to her as if she had intrinsic value, treated her with dignity, took her words seriously, and empowered her to discuss "manly" matters of eternal consequence.

---

foot was catastrophic. For two years, hopeful doctors tried to piece together fragments of the talus bone in her ankle. During two years, ten surgeries, and countless visits to the infectious disease doctor, all attempts to give her a functioning, weight-bearing, infection-free ankle failed. No repairs worked.

During those two years, we were thrilled when she could actually put weight on her foot. And then we'd be devastated when the pain and breaking down of the fusions appeared. Why didn't the surgeries work? Because hidden from sight, buried deep within the bone, was lingering infection. And as long as that infection was there, her ankle could not heal. Her foot looked like a foot. The initial scar wasn't cosmetically disturbing. But she would never have a fully functioning foot as long as the hidden infection lingered in her body, weakening her anklebone, and slowly destroying any possibility of healing.

Ultimately, for my daughter to walk again, the source of the failed healing had to be addressed. Why? Because no amount of antibiotic arrested her infection. That hidden infection stayed hidden. It essentially said to the antibiotic, "Stay away from me. I like the mess I'm creating here. I'm comfortable." So, after two long years, the infection had to be dealt with in a more drastic way. My daughter's foot had to be amputated.

That doesn't sound like healing, does it? But healing is so much greater than the obvious. My daughter can say with full assurance, "I am blessed." Why? Because through all the unknowns, all the long nights, all the unanswered questions, and all the endless days of having her foot determine what she and her family could and could not do, she trusted that God was with her. She didn't know how everything was going to end—if her foot would be viable, if she would ever walk without severe discomfort or a debilitating limp. She never expected that the healing would turn out to be amputation and a prosthetic that allows her to walk without any limp at all. But she knew without a doubt that God was with her through it all.

Going through this experience with my daughter became another picture for me, although now the metaphor was medical. Jesus encouraged me to stop using bandages for my hidden infections. Little infections. Big infections. Little hurts. Big hurts. "Little" sins. "Big" sins. Bandages don't heal. Lists don't heal. Doing good doesn't heal. Even being nice doesn't heal.

What truly *heals?* Getting rid of the infection—no matter how subtle or drastic the action has to be. And Jesus is the one who can accomplish that.

Looking at the encounters Jesus had with women, I found a grace-filled, loving, willing-to-address-the-real-issues, healing, empowering Jesus. When women asked, Jesus healed them. When a woman dared to bring pain that had burdened her for years, Jesus called her "daughter." And he said that her faith—her throwing herself and her ills totally on him—had healed her. She could go on with her life relieved and in peace.

And so, just as Mary pondered "all these things" in her heart, I reread my scripture. I walked along with the women who met Jesus and listened in on their conversations. It was like watching the orchids growing in my yard, opening up in front of me, and eventually allowing me to peer deeply into their mysterious centers and see their hidden beauty and intrigue.

The encounters Jesus had with women captivated my heart because I saw that Jesus doesn't want us to be stuck in unhealthy lives. He wants us to be whole and healed. He wants us to be at peace, always in his presence.

Process and Dig Deeper

1. Do you think women perceive and process life differently than men? If so, how? Are men from Mars and women from Venus?

2. What are some "dos and don'ts" that you grew up with? What are some things other kids could do that you were not allowed to do? (Or vice versa.) Did you question the importance of any rules your mother or father taught you (often with very good intention) as you grew older?

3. Many of us have a hurt done to us in the past, or a self-inflicted pain, or a hidden sin, or a bad attitude deep within that we cover up because it would be embarrassing to discuss. Do you think these things matter to Jesus? If they do, what do you think he would want us to do with them?

4. Do you think it is fair to say that when we cover up hidden things, it affects the way we make our decisions and the way we live? Do you think we sometimes compensate by trying to make ourselves look good?

5. Have you had an experience that became a picture to you of how much Jesus loves you? Just like the author's "garbage can" experience, has God given you pictures of his love for you?

6. Ruth states, "I had heard that 'relationship with Jesus' phrase so often that it had lost its meaning." What, in your thinking and experience, is the meaning of that phrase? Is it based on knowledge or feelings or both? How is this relationship like human relationships? How does it differ?

7. Do the words of Psalm 42:1–2 resonate with you? "As the deer pants for streams of water, so my soul pants for you, O God. My soul thirsts for God, for the living God. When can I go and meet with God?"

8. Have you ever thought of Jesus living in your house, being at work, accompanying you on errands, and doing ordinary things with you? Would being in Jesus' presence all the time make a difference in how you live your life? Would you feel free or would you feel like you "had to be good?" What would happen to you if Jesus told you throughout the day that he loves you? Would that make a difference?

9. Does Jesus' grace empower you? If so, how?

10. When did you feel close to God today? Does it help each day to remember that Jesus is trying to tell you he wants you to be healthy in your emotions, your body, and your soul?

11. If you're living in Jesus' acceptance and freedom, what are you doing today that gives you joy?

1

The Woman with the Bottle of Perfume

On the Art of Lavish Thankfulness

When I began reading scripture as if it were written to me—a woman loved by Jesus himself, a woman whose picture would be on Jesus' refrigerator door—I began to realize that old habits die hard. It was a lot easier to think of somebody else for whom the stories and words of Jesus would be really helpful. It was hard for me, a good girl without a particularly tawdry past, to put myself in the story

I loved the Old Testament stories. I loved the New Testament stories. I was spoon-fed on them from childhood. These were the stories I cut my teeth on. I heard sermons on them and learned from them. But I didn't think the characters in the stories related directly to my story. Moses, Abraham, David, Daniel, and the prophets were often held up as role models. I was told I should imitate the good things they did and avoid the mistakes they made when they were turning from God. I often heard the details of their lives, but I didn't connect the eternal truths of their stories—their internal struggles—to mine. I heard with my head, but my eyes didn't always see and my heart didn't always feel.

Then I began writing stories for children. Stories based on the real lives of heroic characters surviving very difficult tragedies with hope and courage. Compelling people with intense stories. In spite of all the first-person accounts and primary sources I had to work with when writing my stories, my initial critiques were often very similar. My writer's critique group members loved the stories but didn't feel a connection to the characters. My patient friends were honest with me, and they said I held my characters off, looking at them from a distance. As a result, the reader felt little emotional connection to the characters. Not a good thing. With that kind of response, my manuscripts would not be published.

I had to find a way to discover the emotional core of my characters. I did, but it wasn't a particularly pleasant thing to do because it meant going to hidden parts of my own life and processing each character through my own experience. It required finding the places in my own life that connected in some visceral way with the people I was writing about. In doing that, I ended up going to places that I had intentionally and unintentionally concealed. I recollected events in my life I thought I had forgotten. At times I wondered if this was good for me. Why not just let the past be the past? The forgotten the forgotten. Let sleeping dogs lie.

However, that didn't seem to be the way God wanted to work in me. Because in finding those parts of my heart that I had carefully buried, I also found the emotional core of my characters. As an author, I discovered a literary payoff. Suddenly the characters in my stories came alive. It was the visceral power of story. It's the power of one story illuminating another.

That was good for getting books published. But an eternal truth hid in this discovery. When I found those hidden parts within me that connected to my characters and brought them to the light, I found that Jesus wanted to touch those broken parts of me. He wanted to heal those parts. As a result, I began reading my Bible differently. God, in his love, invited me to hold some of the biblical characters close. He invited me to find my story in theirs.

Those characters and stories became God's story intersecting with mine. The raw humanity of the heroes of faith experiencing the wisdom, justice, power, love, compassion, nurturing, and grace of God somehow began intersecting with me. Their stories started informing mine.

But to be honest, to me the Bible sometimes seemed very male-oriented. I heeded my mother's instruction and inserted a "she" or "her" whenever scriptures spoke of "man." And that was okay because truth is truth, and the eternal truths of scripture found in all the stories spoke to my heart. But I wanted to know more.

I loved the teachings of Jesus. I loved the parables. I read and reread Jesus' Beatitudes and the rest of his Sermon on the Mount. Those universal stories and truths touched me deeply. But at some point, I yearned to know how Jesus related to women. I wanted to understand the grace Jesus showed especially to women. I wanted to know what that looked like. Did he relate differently to women than to men? Did his heart connect in unique ways to the heart of a woman? If so, how?

I figured that if God could show me a glimpse of his grace in a pond at the end of my street, then there was probably much more grace for me to discover in the pages of the Gospels. I suspected that the stories of the women who spoke with Jesus could connect, in some way, to my story. And, more importantly, to the love story of Jesus. I didn't know quite how, but I knew I had to search and find out how those familiar stories connected to my story, to the hidden and forgotten corners of my heart.

The New Testament continues the Old Testament story of God's love and care for his people. However, now Jesus becomes the main character connecting his heart to ours. Reconciling humans to God. Reconciling women to God. In order to get the full impact of the story, Jesus might want us to find how our stories connect to the stories of the people he met. As a woman, it helps when we scratch the surface of our own character and find parts of ourselves in all the characters that Jesus encounters. In fact, we miss the grace if we don't, because the story's major focus is about grace. The grace found in a holy God's relationship to us.

To begin, I read the story of the woman who lavishly poured perfume on the head of Jesus. I met a woman who taught me about the lavishness of a grateful spirit. I witnessed a grateful spirit who came face to face with Jesus' extravagant grace.

Have you ever been with a child who, after opening a gift at a birthday party, has to be prompted by his mother to say thank you? Have you ever been with a child who throws their arms around your legs because you brought them something which tickles their fancy? Have you ever received a thank-you note from someone for something you didn't even know you did? Have you ever sat with someone who doesn't know when her next paycheck is coming in, yet shares the delight she felt in being able to tithe her last check? I met several women in the last weeks who joyfully give plenty from their little. They don't have "tithe" on their list of things to do to make Jesus happy. They give because they feel blessed, even beloved.

We receive and give gifts. How we respond to gifts often means more to the giver than the recipient.

When we walk into the story of the woman with the bottle of perfume and allow all of its parts to permeate our parts, we find the grace of Jesus, not only for her but also for us. Alas, we may also recognize ourselves in those who, for their own private reasons, just do not get why she did what she did. Each character embodies characteristics we might see in ourselves. But I believe we find healing when we identify and say out loud where the story fits—even if the truth hurts. Grace finds us when we admit the not-so-nice parts of ourselves. Finding parts of ourselves in the major and minor characters of this story, we see the love of Jesus welcoming us into intimacy with him and encouraging us to touch the fabric of being truly thankful.

And, lo and behold, Jesus invites us to see ourselves embraced by his grace-loaded attitudes as we meet the lavishly thankful . . .

Woman with a Bottle of Perfume

JERUSALEM WAS ABUZZ WITH DRAMA. Leaders quietly plotted to kill Jesus, but because they didn't want to start a riot, they were waiting until after Passover. At least that's what the rumor mill was churning out. Tension mixed with anticipation. Children playing and leaders plotting. I heard the evil they were intending for Jesus, my Lord, and I knew I needed to see him.

> ~
>
> *"I tell you the truth, wherever the gospel is preached throughout the world, what she has done will also be told, in memory of her."*
> —Mark 4:18
>
> ~

Then I heard that Simon had invited Jesus to his home. I didn't know Simon, but somehow, knowing Jesus was going to Simon's house gave me courage to walk alone into a place I had not been invited. I had a gift I wanted to give Jesus because I never had the opportunity to let him know how much his "life-light" meant to me.

I'm not sure Simon knew me, but I knew of him. And although he would probably not want to admit it, he and I had lived similar lives. In a sense, we were both exiles. We were both on the outside looking in—though for completely different reasons and in entirely different venues.

We were both still known by what we had once been.

Simon was still called "Simon the Leper," even though his skin was clear. Even though he no longer had to wear torn clothes. Even though he was no longer required to have uncombed, unwashed hair and a covered face. Even though, when the wind blew, he no longer had to stand at least fifty yards away from those who considered themselves clean.

He was no longer shunned. No longer unclean. He was now allowed to go to temple. He could now live in his home and invite visitors into it. Yet in their minds, he was still "Simon the Leper."

My past life was also known. When they called me "a woman," they remembered what I had been, perhaps with a personal knowledge they hoped others wouldn't recognize. My presence was an embarrassment to many. From some of their mouths, I had heard secrets. I was the unofficial priest for the confessions of many a man who thought I was too stupid to understand and, at the same time, smart enough to know I had no power over them. They misinterpreted my silence for caring. My soulless affection for the salving of their longings. I felt their empty hearts, their greed, their passion for power, their senseless strivings, and their clawing for command. Even though they had wives at home, they came to me for sexual pleasure. No complications. No commitments.

But they didn't understand that, through an encounter with Jesus, I had repented. If repentance means turning around and going the other way, that's exactly what I did. I turned around. I turned off my red light and didn't look back. Jesus, my Lord, gave me a dignity I didn't know I possessed. As demeaning as the life I inflicted on myself was, I have no shame. I'm forgiven. I'm free. I'm valuable. I'm loved. And through my encounter with Jesus, I received a gift from him. A gift no one can buy. Free. No charge. No hourly rate.

But how do you say thank you to someone who leads you on the path toward making everything new in your life? How do you thank someone who helps you see yourself as fresh, clean, and filled with wondrous possibilities for good? As someone who can walk with her head held high?

As I walked the streets of my town, I learned something about how people respond to gifts too costly to purchase.

One day I heard of Jesus healing ten lepers, and only one came back to say thank you. I was astonished.

You know, there are different kinds of thankfulness. I don't know why those nine lepers ran to their Jewish priest to show themselves healed from their awful disease but didn't turn around to first thank the one who had healed them. I guess you can be thrilled that you are no longer plagued with a condition that separates you from others. Happy that you are no longer unclean. Ecstatic that you are now like everyone else. But if you concentrate only on the gift and forget the giver, you wake up some morning and invariably see the wrinkles and the flaws in your healed-from-leprosy skin. You have to run out for more honey and olive oil to make more moisturizing cream. The euphoria of the sensational healing can easily give way to the daily grind of the commonplace.

But I understand the one leper who returned to thank Jesus. His response resonates with how I feel. He wasn't only thankful for the healing, he was thankful to the one who healed him. He celebrated the giver more than the gift. He had an overwhelmingly thankful spirit.

I found out that Jesus not only healed my shamed spirit— and for that I was grateful beyond belief—but he also gave me a healing that spilled over into everything. I was changed and freed. Inside and out. That made a difference in how I lived. Each day was a fresh beginning, a new gift filled with possibilities for really living.

That's why, until they mentioned it, I didn't even think about the cost of the nard that I poured on Jesus' head. The cost was meaningless to me. I only wanted to thank him. I couldn't put a price on the retrieval of dignity Jesus gave me. No appraiser could evaluate what worth means to someone who has felt worthless for as long as she can remember. The value of the pure and without-strings-attached love of Jesus couldn't be put into a column of numbers and added at the end of the year. My forgiveness could not be quantified. There was no money purse large enough to hold the freedom my heart held. My heart was no longer in chains, because Jesus held the key.

When I entered Simon's house, Jesus was reclining on a couch. Some of his disciples and other people were gathered there, and the room was filled with sounds of lively and somewhat confrontational conversation. I worked my way through the crowd, stood beside Jesus, broke the seal of my alabaster bottle, and anointed his head with the expensive oil. All of it. The musky fragrance immediately filled the room.

For a moment there was a stunned silence. And then all I heard was:

"What is she doing?"

"Isn't that just like a woman?"

"Hey, what are you doing?"

"Don't you know how much that costs?"

"Don't you know that's worth a whole year's wages?"

"Why are you wasting the whole bottle?"

"You broke an alabaster bottle."

"You could have given the money you paid for that to the poor."

All the arrows of their jarring accusations were pointed at me, and I felt each one.

Moreover, they didn't get it. They didn't understand.

In fact, even Simon, who had been healed from leprosy and must have been so happy to be back in his home and entertaining friends, didn't get it. He hadn't even bothered to provide water for Jesus to clean his own feet much less get down on his hands and knees and wash Jesus' feet for him. You'd think he would have been the first to say thanks in that way!

They thought I just wasted a lot of money. They accused me of being extravagant. Uncaring towards the poor.

They didn't understand I had no vocabulary large enough to express my gratitude to Jesus. How do you tell someone you now feel alive? That being healed doesn't just happen on the outside where everybody looks, but it also happens in the core of your heart. How could they know I lived every one of my ordinary days as an extraordinary gift? That unashamedly holding my head up and walking into a crowd felt like a celebration. That I had nothing to hide. That I was free. Forgiven. Clean. And grateful beyond words.

That's why I poured the oil on Jesus' head. That's why the perfume mingled with my tears of joy. It was the love offering of my grateful heart—an offering far too small.

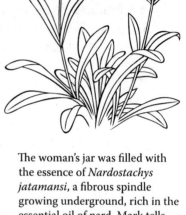

The woman's jar was filled with the essence of *Nardostachys jatamansi*, a fibrous spindle growing underground, rich in the essential oil of nard. Mark tells us the woman brought the oil in a precious alabaster flask, which confirms its significant value. In the Song of Solomon, nard is a symbol of purity. Nard has an exquisite, intense, warm, fragrant, and musky scent, similar to the aromas of humus.

"Leave her alone," Jesus said. "Why are you bothering her? She has done a beautiful thing to me. The poor you will always have with you, and you can help them any time you want. But you will not always have me. She did what she could. She has poured perfume on my body beforehand to prepare for my burial. I tell you the truth, wherever the gospel is preached throughout the world, what she has done will also be told in memory of her."

Suddenly the chorus of accusers stopped their inquisitive chatter.

I had no idea what Jesus meant. "A beautiful thing?" "You will not always have me with you?" "She prepared my body for burial?" "Wherever the gospel is preached what she did will be told in her memory?" Jesus apparently saw much more than I did in that bottle of perfume. He saw some sort of lasting significance in my gift. He saw into the future and claimed my gift to be something of great worth, and I don't think he was talking about the monetary value of that bottled nard.

I did what I needed to do: I thanked Jesus, the giver, for the meaningful and dignified life he gave me. That's what I did on that day in Simon's house and every day since. Just because I love him.

This story was taken from the Gospel of Mark (14:1–11) and Luke (7:36–50).

Process and Dig Deeper

1. Whose pictures do you display in your home or on your refrigerator? Why do we post such pictures and not tuck them away in a drawer? Can you imagine Jesus having your picture on his refrigerator? Why or why not?

2. With whom do you feel a real connection? What does it take for you to trust someone? What is it about that person that allows you to be honest?

3. How can we "scratch the surface of our own character" so that we can begin identifying with the characters in the Bible?

4. How many times does a child's spirit have to be wounded before they believe they are not valuable? How long do those scars last? For a while? Into adulthood? Forever?

5. Simon the Leper was healed from a physical condition. What was the woman's healing? What do you think Jesus might have done or said that changed the whole perspective this woman had about herself? How did Jesus change her life? What was she now free from? What do you think she was now free to be or do?

6. What adjective would you use to describe the woman's action? Do you think her attitude spilled over into the rest of her life?

7. What is the difference between being happy for receiving something and giving thanks to someone? Can you do both? How long does the thrill of a gift last (no matter how badly

you wanted it)? How soon do you put something else on your list? How long do your feelings toward the giver of the gift last?

8. What was a leper's life like in Israel? Why do you think nine of the ten didn't go back to thank Jesus for healing them? Did they think it was enough to follow the command, "Go show yourselves to the priests"—in other words, to do their duty before the law—rather than also going back to say thank you? How did Jesus feel about not being thanked?

9. In what ways were the woman and Simon the Leper similar? How did each respond/relate to Jesus? Why do you think Simon invited Jesus to his home?

10. What were the various responses to the woman's gift? Speculate why the people in the room were so upset with the woman's extravagant giving of thanks. Might similar feelings have crossed your mind when you heard the accusers comment on the cost of her gift?

11. Can you imagine a person today responding to a gift of a spiritual awakening by giving a year's salary as a charitable donation? What would be your first (second, third) response to this?

12. Mark 14:10–11 indicates that the woman's extravagant act was what pushed Judas over the edge. He immediately left and made the deal to betray Jesus (for only thirty pieces of silver) with the chief priests. What might have set him off?

13. Jesus isn't physically in the room with us right now. You can't pour oil over his head to express your thanks. Is it important for us to give thanks? How many different ways can we as twenty-first century women say thanks today for what Jesus' love means to us?

2

If I Were the Woman Who Hemorrhaged for Twelve Years

On Loneliness and Isolation

In Luke 8, we read a desperate woman's story. This woman has battled bleeding issues for twelve years. And we meet her as Jesus is on his way to heal the twelve-year-old daughter of Jairus, a synagogue leader. His little girl has lived the same amount of time that the woman battled her blood issues—twelve years.

The story of this woman overwhelms me. Here I read of Jesus reaching out to one of the most disenfranchised women in town while on his way to help the sick child of an important synagogue leader. In the middle of a pushing and shoving crowd, he senses the heart of a woman who has been ailing and isolated for twelve years.

Isolation is a strange feeling. It's the feeling of walking into a crowd of people you think you know and feeling an impenetrable glass wall around you. You're there. Everybody sees you. But nobody has anything to say to you, and you have nothing to say to anybody. It's being in the middle of a sea of people on an island only large enough for you. It's recognizing faces and not knowing names. It's having a story to tell and nobody in the crowd who might be even remotely interested in hearing it. It's being alone with a problem you're sure no one else can understand. It's being hunkered down in the throes of desperation, not daring to let anyone get to know you because you've been hurt once too often. And sometimes it's being lonely right in your own home, surrounded by your own family.

Sometimes I welcome a self-imposed isolation—for a while. It gives me time to think or process, or just be. Sometimes isolation is necessary for recharging my heart's battery. But an isolation that is imposed upon you, for whatever reason (usually not a good one), is lonely, frightening, judgmental, and desolate.

After I wrote my first book, *Erika's Story*, I heard from many Jewish people who had been in concentration camps—the ultimate isolation here on earth. They were bombarded on every side with the message that they were worthless and despicable. And because of the fate of their birth, they were relegated to camps where Nazis attempted to strip every shred of dignity from them. They were isolated from everything that had, at one time, given their life meaning. When I spoke with one man who called me, I asked him if he wanted to talk about some of his experiences, because so much of what happened had been left unsaid. He said to me, "Ruth, we became like animals. I saw a man fight his son for a piece of bread." What a stark picture of imposed exile's horrible by-products.

Many years ago, I attended a conference where we were grouped with people we didn't know. All day I heard stories of people in my small group who had been, or who currently were, so broken they were hanging on by a thread. But the thread was still there and by the grace of God they were still able to hold on. I didn't have a story like that. And when I told my story, members of the group told me things like how lucky my husband was to have a wife like me. I remember one comment very well: "You are so beautiful." For somebody who never thought she rated very high on the beauty charts, that compliment felt pretty good. I liked that and, in my naiveté, I felt affirmed.

When the conference ended, I was in the lobby, standing alone and waiting for the people who were going to give me a ride home. It was then I noticed the other members of my group still chatting with each other, leaning into each other in conversation, exchanging phone numbers, and talking to each other. When they saw me, they didn't call me over. They had no need to know my phone number because, on some visceral level, we had not connected during the day. All of a sudden, all that affirmation I received seemed pointless and isolating. I felt like a vase on a pedestal, a vase that everyone admired and nobody dared touch.

I have a lot of ways to live through periods of isolation, and none of them are very healthy. "Poor me" and withdrawal come immediately to mind. I guess the bleeding woman's story connects with me on many levels because her possible responses are similar to the responses I might have to an isolating condition. There are lots of "conditions" in the life of a Christian woman. They are the parts of us we don't even know are broken because we have been gluing them together so well for so long. It's the stuff that interferes with us being a whole and healed woman inside and out. It's the stuff we carry around like a sack of rocks because that's what we think we were meant to do. It's the little and big lies we tell so that everyone thinks we are okay. It's the stuff we did and didn't do. The decisions we made and didn't make. The places where we hesitated and the places where we shouldn't have hesitated. It's the stuff we put up with and shouldn't have put up with. And all of this has a way of isolating us in one way or another.

Isolation has a way of distorting reality. It is the "mirror darkly" rather than the clear reflection. Isolation has many negative by-products that create a whole new level of things to deal with. The by-products unhealthily limit and distort our lives.

If I allow myself to honestly feel my isolation and to look closely at all my by-products, I understand the desperateness, admire the determination, share the longing for kindness, and respect the woman who was desperate enough to seek out Jesus.

And I'm grateful for Jesus, who listened to, valued, respected, responded, and blessed the only woman he called . . .

Daughter

If I were the woman who hemorrhaged for twelve years,

- ❧ I might feel tired because of my chronic loss of blood.
- ❧ I might feel destitute because I spent all my money on doctors and they never helped me.
- ❧ I might feel hopeless because my condition seemed to be incurable.
- ❧ I might feel despondent because my "time of the month" never ended.
- ❧ I might feel embarrassed because I could not bear children.
- ❧ I might feel out of control because my body was working against me, and I could do nothing about it.
- ❧ I might feel abandoned because my husband had likely left me because of my condition.
- ❧ I might feel dirty because my culture said I was.
- ❧ I might feel far from God because I could never go to the temple to worship.
- ❧ I might feel isolated because no one could sit in any chair I sat in.
- ❧ I might feel untouchable because that is what I was: No one could touch me or they would be considered unclean and would have to go to the *mikvah* (or small bath) and thoroughly wash themselves in order to become clean again.
- ❧ I might feel used because even though I would be able to touch a child under the age of five without them becoming unclean (I guess they needed child care), I could not touch anyone else.

∾ I might feel taken advantage of because if my husband did stick with me, I could fill his cup, make his bed, wash his hands and feet, and serve him only with my left hand. And for all that, if I had sex with him, he would consider that as having sex with a dead body and then would have to go through purification rites for himself.

∾
"Daughter, your faith has healed you. Go in peace and be freed from your suffering."—Mark 5:34
∾

∾ I might feel emotionally drained because no one could ever touch, kiss, or comfort me.

∾ I might feel jealous because it looked like every other woman had an easier life than mine.

∾ I might feel bitter because the sweetness I dreamed of for my life was never realized.

∾ I might feel sorry for myself because I was lonely and no one seemed to notice.

∾ I might feel angry.

∾ I might feel like a victim because this happened to me

∾ I might feel ashamed.

If I were the woman who hemorrhaged for twelve years,

> And I felt rejected by everyone around me,
> And I was at the end of my rope,

The rectangular prayer shawl *(tallit)* covered the head and shoulders. It had one tassel *(tzitzit)* on each of its four corners.

And I had nowhere else to go,
And I was being devoured by negative feelings,
And I could no longer look anyone in the face,
And I had played out all of my "poor me" behaviors,
And I could no longer find any hope within me,

Then I might make the same decision the woman made.

- ∾ I might believe the rumors about this Jesus who was able to heal and rescue the most ostracized and destitute.
- ∾ I might enter a crowd in which I wasn't welcome.
- ∾ I might push ahead in the crowd, even though by this time everyone in my town knew my condition and knew I didn't belong there.
- ∾ I might press in against all those people, even though, in my heart, I knew they would think I was disgusting.
- ∾ I might trust that touching the tassels on the hem of Jesus' prayer shawl would be enough to send healing to my body.

If I were the woman who hemorrhaged for twelve years,

And I felt rejected by everyone around me,
And I was at the end of my rope,
And I had nowhere else to go,
And I was being devoured by negative feelings,
And I could no longer look anyone in the face,
And I had played out all of my "poor me" behaviors,
And I could no longer find any hope within me,
And I touched the tassel on Jesus' prayer shawl,
And he stopped and turned around and asked who
touched him,

- ∞ I might feel exposed because Jesus talked about my private condition in front of everyone.
- ∞ I might be afraid that Jesus would ridicule me because I had now made him unclean.
- ∞ I might pretend that it wasn't me.
- ∞ I might hide my head in shame.
- ∞ I might think that, just like every other man in my culture, Jesus wanted nothing to do with me.
- ∞ I might be apprehensive, knowing that I was about to be shunned by everyone in that crowd.
- ∞ I might feel worthless and expect nothing.
- ∞ I might suspect that I was certainly not as important to Jesus as Jairus, whose daughter he was on his way to heal.
- ∞ I might be nervous because Jesus' disciples shook their heads and asked, "What do you mean? We're being trampled by a mob and you ask who touched you?"
- ∞ I might be resigned to the fact that I was hopeless.

Each of the four tzitzit (tassels) was white and included at least one blue cord. The tassels helped the wearer remember God's commands (Num. 15:38–39).

If I were the woman who hemorrhaged for twelve years,

> And I felt rejected by everyone around me,
> And I was at the end of my rope,
> And I had nowhere else to go,
> And I was being devoured by negative feelings,
> And I could no longer look anyone in the face,
> And I had played out all of my "poor me" behaviors,

And I could no longer find any hope within me,
And I touched the tassel on Jesus' prayer shawl,
And he stopped and turned around and asked who touched him,
And I felt my private condition exposed in front of everyone,
And I was afraid how Jesus would respond,
And then I heard him call me "Daughter,"

- ✑ I would be amazed at his gentleness.
- ✑ I would feel overwhelmed by his kindness.
- ✑ I would be reassured by Jesus' words because I would know that I wasn't in trouble for touching him.
- ✑ I would appreciate that he wasn't patronizing and making me feel like some poor, sick, desperate woman.
- ✑ I would feel as important as Jairus when Jesus talked to me immediately and didn't demand that I make an appointment.
- ✑ I would feel empowered that he congratulated me on my audacity to touch him.
- ✑ I would be so thankful for the healing I immediately knew happened in my body.
- ✑ I would suddenly realize that it took a lot of faith for me to do what I did. And that my life was changed forever. And that I was a new woman.

If I were the woman who hemorrhaged for twelve years,

And I felt rejected by everyone around me,
And I was at the end of my rope,
And I had nowhere else to go,
And I was being devoured by negative feelings,
And I could no longer look anyone in the face,
And I had played out all of my "poor me" behaviors,

And I could no longer find any hope within me,
And I touched the tassel on Jesus' prayer shawl,
And he stopped and turned around and asked who
touched him,
And I felt my private condition exposed in front of
everyone,
And I was afraid how Jesus would respond,
And I heard him call me "Daughter,"
And knew that I was healed,

∽ I would understand that it was Jesus who was able to
heal me, body and spirit, so that I could live.
∽ I would understand that I became hopeful after I admitted my hopelessness.
∽ I would understand that peace came to me when I
risked trusting in Jesus.
∽ I would understand that I became dignified when I
humbled myself.
∽ I would understand that I was free.
∽ I would understand that the negative feelings I held on
to needed as much healing as my body.
∽ I would understand that Jesus showered grace over me
and helped me feel clean.
∽ I would understand that no games I play will heal my
hurts. No feeble attempts on my part to feel accepted
by others will heal my emotions. No manipulation of
people or circumstances will help me feel included.
∽ I would understand I live free, clean, confident, hopeful, and, yes, included—only because I took a risk and
trusted that just by touching the tassel on the hem of
Jesus' prayer shawl, I would be healed.
∽ And I could go in peace.

This story is taken from the Gospel of Luke (8:40–49).

Process and Dig Deeper

1. Have you ever felt alone in the middle of a group of people you somewhat knew? If so, what do you do then?

2. Are there times when being alone is a good thing? If so, when and why? When does isolation become lonely and unproductive?

3. What were the cultural, religious, and social reasons the bleeding woman probably lived a very isolated life?

4. What were the reasons from within her heart that probably caused her to live a very isolated life?

5. What does this story tell us about Jesus' regard for all people in the desperateness of their situations (for Jairus and his daughter as well as the woman)?

6. If you had been in the woman's situation, how difficult might it have been for you personally to "expose" twelve years of isolation in front of the crowd?

7. How do you think the woman felt when Jesus called her "Daughter"? What does that name mean to you?

8. How did the woman experience the grace of Jesus? What were the effects of that grace in her life?

9. There were many self-imposed and external hurdles this woman had to overcome in order seek out Jesus. Do you think her efforts were driven by desperation or a faith that Jesus

could help her? What role do faith and trust in God (Jesus) play in restoring peace and wholeness in our lives?

10. The woman in this story expressed many feelings: tired, destitute, hopeless, despondent, out of control, embarrassed, abandoned, dirty, far from God, isolated, untouchable, used, taken advantage of, emotionally drained, jealous, bitter, sorry for herself, angry, victimized, ashamed, rejected, at the end of her rope, nowhere else to go, devoured by negative feelings, poor-me attitudes, exposed, afraid, pretending it wasn't her, hiding her head in shame, apprehensive, worthless, ostracized, unwelcome, didn't belong, disgusting, nervous, resigned to the place she was. Which of these describes you?

11. Do you understand this woman? Do you connect with her even though it might be for different reasons? How would you feel if you heard Jesus call you "Daughter"? What would his voice sound like? What would it be like to experience the grace of Jesus when you feel some of those miserable feelings?

12. What have you learned for your own life from this woman's story?

3

I Only Wanted the Best for My Sons

On Letting Go So Our Children Can Flourish

I was raised on Chicago's south side.

I played outside with the neighbor kids until the nighttime streetlights came on.

One summer afternoon, I sneaked the five blocks away from home to play by the train tracks, and by the time I got home, everybody within a three-block radius had told my mom where I was. I didn't play outside the rest of that night. The kids played right in front of my house and informed everyone that I was in trouble.

From September to June, I walked the mile to and from school with those same kids every day.

In the mid-1960s, after marrying Vern, fresh out of seminary, we moved to Los Angeles to serve a church in a community where the neighborhood was changing. This was right after the Watts riots, when racial feelings ran high and people were desperately and often angrily trying to understand each other. Or not. We found ourselves in the middle of a mix of heated discussions, compassionate acts of kindness, stubborn refusals to accommodate, and gracious hospitality. Community empowerment and defeat lived side by side.

Five years later, we moved to a bedroom community of San Francisco. My children changed buses at the congested BART (Bay Area Rapid Transit) station on their way to school, and the boys skateboarded through the many neighborhoods in that beautiful Pacific coast city. Our church was a mix of people with long histories in our denomination, people who knew nothing of the denomination but loved the church, and neighbors immigrating into the country from Asia, seeking a place where they felt loved and respected.

Later we lived in a western suburb of Chicago, serving a church with a long history, strong loyalties, and relationships that wove through each other to the third and fourth generations.

And now we serve in culturally diverse Miami, the adopted home of many people from Latin and South America and all points east and west. Our church members have their roots in over thirty-two different countries.

All of these cities can be, and often are, reduced to caricatures of themselves because they each have distinctive identities. All of the churches we served have their own characteristics and a basic DNA which runs through their very being. Each of the cities is complex, and each church unique. They are all very different from each other. Each has its own sensibilities, politics, and issues. Yet they all have some things in common. They are filled with people who are living in community, sometimes understanding each other, and sometimes scratching their heads at one another. At times living together peacefully, and at other times sowing and reaping discord.

In this chapter, we meet Salome, the mother of James and John, and her common motherly request. You can plop her in any city, in any church, in any family. We know her. Citizens of Los Angeles, San Francisco, Miami, and all large and small towns in between hear this story and find themselves in it. Churches in countries near and far, from east to west and north to south, resonate with the truths in this story. Families understand this story. Friends get it. We live with people like her. Sometimes we *are* her.

This is the story of Anytown. It's a story about neighbors. It's a story about family. It's a story about relationships. No matter how large or small the city in which we live, or our family or the friends we spend time with, we soon know what to expect. We learn our place in the pecking order. We know who we can depend on to always say this or that, do this or that, or think this or that.

And as annoying or good as that can be, depending on your point of view, it's what we know. It's comfortable. We learn to deal with it, and we weave our lives around what we expect to happen in our little corner of the world. We know our place and so does everybody else.

We know who looks out for us, who covers our backs, and who will give us a pat on the back. Who will be the first to gossip or give an opinion, who has good words of advice, and who will throw out a cynical remark or an off-color joke. We know who is likely to slip us some money and who will probably tell us we were irresponsible. Who will get angry or take offense, and who will tell us to get over it or sympathize. All of this and more becomes the rhythm of a community. The fabric of our lives. It's what we learn in order to survive in community.

If we respond unexpectedly with a new attitude—we're suddenly not the cheery person we always were, or we're positive when we have always been critical—we wreak havoc with the community's equilibrium. Communities, no matter how large or small, don't do well with the unexpected. They're quite sure the next shoe will drop and, when it does, it isn't going to be good. Changes make communities nervous. They aren't sure how to respond.

Jesus experienced this kind of reaction when as an adult he returned to Nazareth to heal and to prophesy. The kid he played with on the school playground was suspicious of him. He bewildered the girl who had a crush on him in fourth grade. The mother who chased him out of her newly planted garden when he trampled her fledgling anemones wasn't going to take such unexpected behavior from him. After all, they knew Jesus' father was a carpenter. They knew his brothers and sisters. Why should Jesus suddenly come as a prophet and healer into the community in which he was raised? Or talk to neighbors about the kingdom of God? That didn't make sense, upsetting what they knew of how their community worked. Jesus understood this and acknowledged that a prophet was without honor in his own community. After all, what could he tell them? So Jesus stopped healing and laid hands only on those who were open to his healing touch.

But Jesus is Lord of the Community of New Responses. His Spirit prompts us to tweak the way we usually and expectedly look at our world. Sometimes I like the way I respond, knowing it comes generously from my heart. Sometimes I'm ashamed of my responses because they come from an unlovely place. And sometimes I'm surprised by my own responses. There are times when I'm with people from my community who I have known for a long time—I know what to expect from them and what to expect from myself when I'm with them—and something startling happens. One of us changes. One of us responds unexpectedly. One of us chooses to reveal a fresh dimension of Jesus in them, and then we all inexplicably change. That's often when we feel the power of a new beginning. A new response. And those changes are often grace-filled kingdom living at its best.

Maybe this is why I begin to see the kingdom of God as a place of new responses when I hear it through Jesus' aunt, who thought she had every right to say . . .

I Only Wanted the Best For My Sons

MY NAME IS SALOME and I learned that children do not come with instruction manuals. In fact, my sister and I learned that lesson very well. But sometimes it takes almost a lifetime to figure out the ramifications of that truth.

I know you're well acquainted with my sister—Mary, the mother of Jesus. I have lived in her shadow for many years. She had the extraordinary experience of being visited by an angel and being told, before she was married, that she was pregnant with the Son of God. Her life has been a roller-coaster ride ever since.

> *"You don't know what you are asking. . . .Can you drink the cup I am going to drink?" —Matt. 20:22*

We, along with our husbands, were raising our children as best we knew how, learning as we went along. Mary was the wife of Joseph, a respected carpenter, so their son, Jesus, spent many hours perfecting the carpentry trade alongside his father. Meanwhile, twenty-five miles away, I lived with my fisherman husband, Zebedee. He owned boats, and my boys learned to fish on the Sea of Galilee. They learned to sense when the storms stirred up that sea. Learned the best fishing spots. Learned to mend nets.

Both Mary and I were relieved we had done our duty as wives to bring sons into the world, guaranteeing our family's financial security. We watched our sons grow. They brought us the usual joys and worries.

Talk about worries. I fretted over my sons out on the sea, though they usually stayed with their father. But Mary! Mary had worries I never even considered. She was a remarkable mother, but sometimes I wonder if she understood who Jesus really was. How could she? How could any of us? She was raising a son who was similar to every other child and yet like no other child. She was raising an extraordinary son in the middle of her exceedingly ordinary life.

I think she recognized greatness in her son and yet had no idea what she was supposed to do to nurture him. To teach and to mold him. To train him. How could she herself prepare her son for the tasks the angel spoke of before his birth?

And perhaps that is why she and Joseph were so diligent about teaching Jesus the stories and celebrations of our heritage. The story of God's mercy to our people. The story of God's promises—of his faithfulness.

~

Mary, Joseph, and Jesus walked 140 miles back and forth from Nazareth to Jerusalem in order to celebrate Passover.

Each Passover began on the fifteenth day of the month of Nissan to commemorate the Jews' exodus from Egypt after four hundred years of slavery.

Passover lasted for seven days, with no work permitted on the first and last days of that week.

A special family meal *(Seder)*, filled with rituals that remind everyone of the significance of the holiday, was shared on the first night of Passover. No yeast was used to prepare bread during Passover.

~

It was part of their family's yearly pilgrimage to walk 140 miles back and forth from Nazareth to Jerusalem in order to celebrate the Passover. They obeyed the instructions given to us long ago and observed the ceremony. Faithfully. Jesus grew up making that trek. He knew the way.

So I was speechless when Mary told me what happened at the Passover celebration the year Jesus turned twelve. Mary and Joseph walked back toward home and realized they hadn't seen Jesus for a while. They assumed he was playing around with his friends and didn't worry. But after a while, when they looked and didn't find him, they became frantic, turned around, and trekked all the way back to Jerusalem. They did what I would have done. They first looked in all the normal places a kid would go. They looked for three days! When they were completely sick with worry, they went to the last place they would have thought to look and found him there—in the temple.

That's where he was. Sitting in the temple, listening to the teachers, and asking them questions. Mary told me Jesus didn't seem at all aware that she and Joseph might be concerned. They had been looking for him for three days, and all that time, he was sitting in the temple with men older than his father, discussing as if he were one of them.

Now I know my sons; they wouldn't have had the patience to sit that long anywhere and especially in the temple talking to teachers. My sons worked with their hands. Outside. They needed to be active and didn't have the patience to sit still.

But there was Jesus, in the temple. And he wasn't talking only to the teachers and asking them very good questions, but he was also contributing to the conversation. Mary told me that the men there were amazed. He was only twelve years old, and he could keep up with them, asking good questions and giving his own insights.

Mary said she was beyond bewildered. She was exhausted after walking all those miles, losing her son, and then searching around the area for three days. I know I would have been furious if James and John had done that to me. I guess I would have said pretty much the same thing she said to Jesus: "Why in the world did you treat us like this?"

After all, whether angels really visited her during her pregnancy or not, Jesus was still her only son and he was only twelve years old. But do you know what he then said to Mary? "Why are you looking for me? Don't you know I have to be about my Father's business?"

At that, Mary looked at her son and realized something. She knew him—and yet didn't really know him. Father? He had a father. Jesus worked side by side with him every day. Business? His father had a business and it wasn't in the temple. It was carpentry.

I would have been thoroughly confused by all the reality Mary encountered in those few minutes. Wondering what her son knew about himself. Wondering what she, as his

mother, was supposed to do with such a son. She was a pon-
dering woman, my sister Mary. But she carried on.

And I have to say, Jesus didn't complain. He went back
home with Mary and Joseph, and he returned to work with
Joseph in the shop.

But as our boys grew older, I watched Jesus. He was a bit
of a puzzle to me. There was something about him that made
him different than my boys.

That is why, when he became an itinerant rabbi at the age
of thirty, I kept an eye on the news passed along by travel-
ers. Our country was under Roman rule and we had horrible
political issues to deal with. Jesus seemed to be a leader and
one who attracted attention. I don't know if I ever recognized
him as a political leader, although secretly I thought he could
be the answer to all the miserable Roman oppression. But he
obviously was strongly committed to his emerging ministry.

Jesus eventually left Joseph's carpentry business. And let
me tell you, I had grave misgivings when he asked my sons
to leave their father's fishing business. But James and John
didn't think twice. They dropped everything and left. My
husband, Zebedee, was remarkable. He let his sons, his best
helpers, go with Jesus. With his blessing!

Now, I have to say, even though I wasn't sure about all
this, I was proud of my family's commitment. Even Jesus'
own brothers didn't follow him. But my James and John did.
One minute they were fishing on the Sea of Galilee with their
father, and the next minute they were following their cousin
all over land and sea.

When they traveled, I didn't go with them. But my husband was very open to me following Jesus and my boys when
they were in town. The longer I followed, the more I believed
that Jesus was up to something great. He was an amazing
teacher. It felt odd to be taught by my nephew, but I wanted
to be with my sister and my boys, so I followed. And what

I saw and heard was different than what I had heard before. Jesus often told variations of the same stories I had heard from the rabbis, but his stories often had a different twist. They were filled with love and grace.

Unfortunately, most people remember me for the foolish request I made. I don't know if you have ever lived with the consequences of one stupid remark that hangs around for the rest of your life, but I have. I said what I did because I lacked peace about my sons' futures. I thought Jesus might overlook them, and I didn't want that for them. After all, my family gave up a lot for my James and John to be with Jesus. Those three young men were very close and really loved each other. But I felt like my husband and I suffered a bit because the boys were gone so much of the time.

It became evident to me that Jesus was on the cusp of becoming the leader of a great political upheaval. We were so sick of Roman occupation. Their rules, taxation, and military presence in our country were very troublesome. We yearned for release from their oppression. It seemed Jesus was gathering political clout. I hoped he would be the new leader who could get our land back. I knew there was a lot of dissent about what he was doing, but in spite of that, I believed he could pull it off.

So I talked to James and John. I felt they should have a place of honor in Jesus' future government, and I encouraged them to ask him for such a position when he established his kingdom. After all, they were cousins. They had supported

Salome was far from her home and in unfamiliar territory when she made her request to Jesus.

She lived in Capernaum on the northern end of the Sea of Galilee.

She was now sixty miles south of her home on a trip toward Jerusalem (in southern Palestine).

She stayed on for Passover in Jerusalem. Unexpectedly for her, this trip also included Jesus' crucifixion and resurrection.

Jesus' Passover meal with his disciples became the New Testament Lord's Supper.

him from the beginning of his ministry and really got along well together. In situations like this, I think blood is thicker than water. Wouldn't Jesus be much better off with family as his closest advisors? James and John agreed with me. And I just wanted to do right by my boys. We had all sacrificed, and it just seemed to me Jesus could show his appreciation that way.

I went to Jesus and asked him to remember my boys when he established his government. I suggested he let them be his closest advisors. You know, one on his right hand and the other on his left. I knew my sons were honest and good men, and when you're establishing a government, you want people like that around you.

But I felt a little put down when Jesus told me I didn't understand my own request. He asked me if they would be willing to drink the cup he was going to drink. I didn't know what he was talking about—drinking out of cups. What could that mean?

He said he didn't have anything to do with who would sit at his side: his Father had prepared the places on his right and left hand. His words really confused me. And then he said his government would be one of servanthood. He said the least would be the greatest and the greatest the least.

Now I was no political expert, but it seemed to me, when I looked around, that powerful governments were not run by servants. Jesus pointed out that the Gentiles lord over everyone. Well, I couldn't agree more. That was our complaint. But when you're in power, what else do you do?

Then he talked about giving his life as a ransom for many.

I felt bewildered. I didn't know what was going on anymore. Sometimes kids amaze you, and you wonder where they learn the things they know. Jesus was my nephew and sometimes I looked at him and wondered where he got his abilities. No one in our family talked like him. We were common folk. I was embarrassed by my apparent lack of understanding about what was going on, and I gave up on asking Jesus to give my boys a place of honor.

But then everything changed. Jesus' life took an unexpected turn. And everything I figured I could do to make things right for my boys seemed so insignificant. We had all heard the rumors. The rumblings came from all around: the religious leaders planned on getting rid of Jesus. Killing him.

All the rumors came true.

That Sunday before Jesus' death was the beginning of a week that changed my life. I, Salome, who prided myself on always being on top of things; who thought ahead so nothing surprised me; who dropped everything to help others; I was helpless.

My boys and I were there that Sunday when the crowds hailed Jesus as the new king and then when they killed him on Friday. I stood at Jesus' cross with my sister. I wept when I saw Jesus suffer. He didn't deserve it! I heard him ask my son John to take care of my sister, Mary. Jesus cried out, "My God, my God why have you forsaken me?" The words pierced my heart. I witnessed him give his life as that ransom he talked about. I watched as he drank the cup. And I knew then I would never understand Jesus "being about his heavenly Father's business." How could I? If I lived a thousand years, I would never understand that kind of selfless love and personal responsibility.

But everything changed. *I* changed.

Mary and I went to the tomb on Sunday morning and saw it was empty. We believed Jesus rose from the dead. The days that followed were a whirlwind of new experiences. That's when I met Jesus, not as my nephew who might get my country out of a political mess, not as a wandering twelve-year-old who gave his mother plenty of reason to worry, but as Jesus my Savior and Lord. Jesus' ministry, teachings, death, and resurrection became personal to me. They changed me forever.

And that cup? I thought about that cup ever since Jesus mentioned it. For me, sitting with a friend, drinking a cup of pomegranate tea soothes my spirit. Lifting that cup, tipping the hot liquid into my mouth, tasting the hint of the fruit, and allowing the tea to be a conduit of friendly chatter and shared intimacies is a beautiful thing. King David said that his cup ran over, and that cup-of-joy image always spoke to me.

But Jesus wasn't talking about cups of joy. I found out his cup was a cup of suffering. The suffering of loneliness, humiliation, abandonment, isolation, and ultimately, death. We all experience those things to greater or lesser degrees. We don't get through life without human trials. But Jesus endured these sufferings in a way unlike I or any of my friends would ever experience them.

Jesus didn't taste sips of suffering; he completely drained the cup. There never was nor will there ever be a putrid, ugly, degrading, stench-filled, gut-wrenching, dark, chaotic, fearful, raucous, thirsty cup like Jesus drank. Never. No one could drink that much. No human could drink that for anyone else. But Jesus did. And that cup became the cup of hope for every human who chooses to share a small part in it. The salvation in his cup came at the highest price possible.

That's where I met the grace of Jesus. He asked me that tough question, "Do you know what you are asking?" And he didn't answer it then. He allowed me to experience my life and let me see his love for me. He allowed me to face my well-intentioned mothering. He didn't scold me. He asked the question that begged a real answer. What was I asking?

And that's when I found out my sons no longer belonged to me. I didn't own them. They were on loan. They walked with Jesus and, as a result, had a calling from God. They had their own cups. None of my selfish ambition or interference could keep God from doing what he intended with them, as long as they were obedient. By letting my sons go, I discovered that they were best able to grow into their full potential. I discovered the obvious; I could see the present, but God knew the future. He knew what my sons would do with their lives. And because they, too, met Jesus as their Savior and Lord, they had a passion for ministry which blessed many. They ministered in the name of Jesus and suffered for him. My John was imprisoned and my James was executed.

That was one of the cups I had to bear. I learned to get rid of the rosy, dancing-in-the-daisies dream of life I thought I could manipulate. I accepted life as it came with all of its stuff—the good and the bad—because I knew who held me safe. I learned I didn't have to be ashamed of what life threw at me but, in Jesus' love, I looked truthfully at it.

So now when I sip a cup of tea with my friend, I realize that we share, in some small way, in the cup Jesus drank. Because of what he did, I share in a community of friends who encourage each other even when we make stupid statements and express uninformed opinions. The suffering in the bitter cup Jesus drank gave me hope because there was also healing there. The pain in that cup gave me peace because there was salvation there.

As I said, my name is Salome. It means peace. When Jesus turned to me and asked the hard question, he made me think. And his question started me on the road to the peace of release. The peace of his grace. Peace in trusting that Jesus accomplished what he was sent by his Father to do so that I could live—really live. Peace to receive the power to be who I was created to be. Peace to let him lead my sons into the place they needed to be in order to serve him. Peace to realize my reality isn't to be coerced by me. Peace to accept the fact that my sons didn't need an overprotective mother who arranged for their good. Peace to know that real power is not politics and control, but service.

He urged me to accept what I could not do. Could not change. Could not control. Could not fix. And peace was mine, not because I had a step-by-step instruction manual for life, but because I trusted in the very cup my faithful Savior and Lord Jesus drank.

This story was taken from the Gospel of Matthew (20:20–28).

Process and Dig Deeper

1. What kind of community were you raised in? What were some of the things you knew you could expect from people in your community? Your home? Your church? Your neighbors?

2. If you have left your community, do you feel different when you go back? Is it still "home"? If you have stayed in your community, do you have the same place in it you always had?

3. Do you think Mary felt pressure being the mother of Jesus? Describe how you picture the relationship between Mary and Jesus when he was a teen. Easy or difficult for Mary? For Jesus?

4. Do you have some sympathy for Salome, who only wanted the best for her sons? What kind of sacrifice did she and Zebedee make in having their sons leave the business? Is it understandable that she would ask Jesus for a favor?

5. Have you talked to God about those you love? How long do you keep talking/asking? How do you know you're asking the right question or for the best outcome? Has God answered your request? Are you still waiting? Are you questioning his answer?

6. Salome lived in tumultuous political times—Jesus was causing a stir and faced considerable opposition. Why do you think Salome went down to Jerusalem with her sister, Mary? Do you think she thought Jesus would be a victorious leader? Do you think she sensed trouble? What feelings might lead a mother to go these distances?

7. When is it good to enter into the lives of grown children, nieces, nephews, or grandchildren with advice or insights?

8. If you're a mother, is it hard to release your children to make their own mistakes or decisions? If you do make suggestions, what worthy justification do you employ?

9. What are some of the ripple effects of hanging on to our kids? Does good come from letting go? Something less than good? Does peace come from letting go? How? Of what? Do you think Salome felt peace?

10. How did Salome change throughout the events in this story? When, how, and why would you guess Salome changed?

11. We know Jesus wants to tell us how much he loves us in all of his encounters. Where is the love and grace and peace for you in this story?

4

Just Plain Mary— Part 1

On How Jesus Can Transform the Broken to Whole

When you grow up, you learn about life from a host of people who in turn learned about life from their own predecessors. All this learning gets sifted through a grid of rightness and wrongness. There are right ways to do your hair, wear your clothes, celebrate your birthdays, speak up, sit down. You learn how clean is clean, what isn't anywhere close to clean, what colors to paint a room, and what colors you never use to decorate a room. You find out who is a show-off, who is humble, and which attitude is better. You're taught what you can do on Sunday and what you can't do on Sunday, which wine to serve at dinner or no wine, ever. How late to let the kids stay up, how to potty train, and whether to use a pacifier with the baby. Which political party is best. Whether to go to work even when you're sick or stay home because you'll make others sick. The list goes on.

Some things are right and some things are wrong—depending on what subset of people you spend time with. Growing up, we often think what we are taught is always correct. And we think if we lived that right way, God would be happy and we would live happily ever after. That thinking becomes lodged pretty deeply in our hearts, and it becomes the lens through which we judge much that happens around us.

And then, just around the corner, Jesus redefines "rightness." In fact, Jesus startles me sometimes. I'm not so sure he is even concerned about rightness. Each time he strips away my holy perceptions of what is right thinking or doing, I'm surprised to discover a whole new level of grace.

Here I am, born into a Christian family. I prayed my evening prayers at my father's knee until I persuaded my parents I was old enough to pray them all by myself in my bedroom. I went to Sunday school every week. Attended Christian schools. Part of the genetic code on my DNA is an awareness of God the Father as my creator and provider, Jesus as my Savior, and the Holy Spirit as the power within me. I was taught this. I listened. I willingly participated in a community which accepted the reality of God the Father, Jesus, and the Holy Spirit. The people in that community based their lives on how they understood that truth.

It was a comfortable community. Its understanding of God was as solid and sure as a rainbow shining during a sunny, summer shower. And my father pointed out every one of them, explaining to me that rainbows reminded God that he would never forget his promise.

I was taught. I listened. I learned. And I thought all of these "right things" pleased God. And I'm still sure they do. However, you can get stuck in rightness. You can be so busy being right that you miss the real story of how to truly live.

I didn't think much about transformation as I grew. From my childhood point of view, it seemed that adults knew what was going to happen, and what they planned is what always happened. Life seemed linear—one step after another—toward a sure end. And that's how I thought my life would unfold. I didn't have great expectations. I had expected expectations. I thought I would grow up, get a job, go to college if I were lucky, get married, have three or four kids, and live happily ever after. And if I weren't really content, or if my kids messed up, or my husband or I had dark secrets, I would never talk about them. I would simply put up with them. I would just need to take one predictable step after another.

I never realized God was in the business of transforming the lives of both the happy and the unhappy, the conventional and the unconventional, the have-it-all-together people and the messed-up ones. I didn't understand that he worked in those who towed the line as well as those who crossed the line, the repaired ones and the broken ones, the open couples or the ones who harbored secrets. I thought you lived your life and, if you messed up, you pretended like nothing was wrong, moved to the sidelines, lived in the shadows, or quietly left town.

I remember walking into the kitchen of my girlfriend's house when my mom and several of her friends were having coffee together. Their heads were bent together and they were talking in hushed tones about another friend who was going through a divorce. In my community, that was the "Big D" word. Nobody divorced. At least it seldom happened. And when and if anyone did, it became the couple's identifying mark. When my mom and her friends saw me, they all stopped talking at once and quickly changed the subject. When I asked about it later, my mom brushed me off a bit and told me it wasn't something to talk about.

I don't know what happened to this woman. I don't even know who she was. But I'm quite sure the pain of her journey wasn't held up as an opportunity for God's grace to be seen in her. No one in my childhood pointed out the possibility that because of her pain or hurt she had the potential to become a hero in the kingdom of God.

That's why Mary Magdalene was so mind-boggling in my childhood perception of step-by-step right living. She had no prayers at her father's knee. No catechism classes. No solid community. All she had to go on was the experience of seven demons inhabiting her spirit and the transforming work of Jesus who noticed and healed her. How did she have the confidence and freedom, with only demons as her tutor, to know and use her spiritual gifts? What inspired her to live a passionate, free, unconventional, no-holds-barred life?

I'm humbled because I thought I knew the right way. I thought it was my solid, sure, linear living. I thought it was the safety and security of one sure step after another. But it's not.

It's my neighbor Jim on Kay Avenue in California. A man who, in trying to please and find favor in the eyes of his dead father, drank himself into a stupor any time he was off work. The afternoon his wife called and asked us to help get Jim to the hospital, I honestly thought I would never see him again. His body was so compromised with alcohol that he could not even sign his own name. Under the glaring lights of the hospital admissions room, I knew I was saying goodbye to Jim.

But God went with Jim into that hospital, and he emerged a transformed person. He was unleashed from the compulsion to drink, and for the next five years of his life he served as an ambassador of the Lord in our church and on our block.

Soon afterward, Jim began feeling badly and found out that he had throat cancer. After a while, the only thing he could stand to swallow was lukewarm coffee and aloe. One morning I went out to the front porch to get the morning paper and found a coffee cup there. Somehow I knew it was Jim's. Sure enough, after about a half hour, he knocked on the door and asked if coffee was on.

He sat at my kitchen table littered with cereal boxes, school lunches, and piles of last night's homework, telling me about the roses he had seen on the next block, the birds he heard singing, the way one of the neighbors cared for his lawn—things he had never seen or heard before. A few months earlier, he would never have had the patience to sit at my table, amid my children's morning chatter and mess, chatting about flowers and birds. But God had transformed his alcohol-drenched heart, and morning after morning Jim blessed my family with his litany of praise. Those were sacramental moments of grace for me.

Jesus transformed Jim's heart. And our Lord does the same for each of us if we let him. He can change our ordinary and our extraordinary, our lovely and our not-so-lovely, our past and our present into something useful and beautiful and purposeful. That's why I love hearing Mary tell me her story of a rescued, recovered, and reclaimed life in . . .

Just Plain Mary–Part 1

YOU CALL ME MARY MAGDALENE. But my name is just plain Mary. I come from Magdala, a beautiful city on the western shore of the Sea of Galilee.

Fishermen came to my town with their boats loaded with fish. The men in my town salted their fish in order to flavor and preserve it. As a matter of fact, my town is called the Fish Tower in the Jewish Talmud.

> *Jesus said to her,*
> *"Mary."*
> *She turned toward him and*
> *cried out in Aramaic,*
> *"Rabboni!"*
> *—John 20:16*

Magdala was a beautiful city. But I never really saw it, even though I lived there. It was on a sea I never enjoyed, even though I could see it from my window. I didn't see, I didn't enjoy, and I didn't feel because my heart was an all-consuming darkness. That's the only way I can describe it. I was filled with confusion, fear, and despair. I constantly felt sad and alone. You know me as the woman who had seven demons.

Demons. I don't know how my heart willingly hosted seven demons. Slowly, I guess. Little by little I was eaten up by everything unlovely and impure. I didn't let go of envy or jealousy. I hung on to those demons and even defended their presence in my life. I was mad at people who didn't do what I wanted. I could feel my blood pressure rising daily, but I thought I had every right to be irate. Nobody understood how deeply I had been wronged. Anger and depression lived right next to each other in my heart.

Demons are fallen angels known as evil spirits. They are Satan's agents, tempting us to commit specific sins. They actively distort and disrupt our relationship with Jesus.

That relationship suffers when we allow any of what are historically known as the seven deadly sins—anger greed, laziness, pride, lust, envy, and gluttony—to lodge comfortably in our hearts.

Satan sends his demons to seduce our hearts, wooing us into excuses to hold onto these sins as if we, of all women in the world, have a right to them.

When these demons convince us to hold on to a sin and we allow the sin to become part of the fabric of our lives, we are oppressed and can come dangerously close to being possessed.

I satisfied myself by eating and eating and eating—everything that wasn't nailed down. "Comfort food," I called it. When I felt like I was losing control, I shopped and ran up debts I couldn't pay. I felt sad when other women had things I didn't have. I didn't feel like working, but that didn't matter. If I flirted enough or used my charms, I could get my creditors off my back. I don't know where I learned such skills, but I wasn't going to let anybody or anything get the better of me. I had my pride, after all.

I cried a lot. As if I were lost. Internal forces pushed and shoved me around. It was as if there were voices inside calling me in a million different directions. At other times, I felt numb and exhausted. I was sure I was fine, but friends avoided me, even gave up on me. I was a lost cause, lonely and miserable.

My heart was chained and I was desperate. And then . . . Jesus healed me.

He poured light into my heart. I felt it.
I calmed down.

I felt peace.
I was joyful.

The things that annoyed me, bothered me, made me angry, and tempted me were still in my life, but they didn't control me. Their power over me was gone. I was

Buoyant.
Euphoric.
Excited.

I couldn't keep my mouth shut about my healing. I told everybody I met.

A funny thing happened about this same time. I heard Jesus tell a story about an evil spirit coming out of a man and going through arid places seeking rest. When the evil spirit didn't find rest, it said, "I will return to the house I left." But when it arrived, it found the house swept clean and put in order. Then it went and found seven other spirits more wicked than itself, and they went in the house together.

I knew what it was like to be cleansed of something terrible. And I was tempted, no, determined to keep my heart cleaned, scoured, and polished. I was willing to work diligently to have a pure heart. I wanted that space in my heart once filled with seven demons to be empty of everything so that I could keep my oh-so-happy feeling.

But, you know, that's a trap. I soon learned the same thing as the man in Jesus' story. An empty heart—no matter how clean—is a breeding ground. It wants to be filled with something. Believe me, I couldn't even imagine getting rid of seven demons and then having forty-nine more come back. But I came kind of close.

It wasn't until I realized that not only had Jesus healed me and cleaned me up that I discovered he also affected my spirit. You might call that the Holy Spirit. I didn't know who the Holy Spirit was, but I knew something important had transformed my heart.

Here I was, just plain Mary, all cleaned up on the inside. I was feeling so good, and, I have to say, looking kind of good on the outside also—it's amazing what happens to your outside when your inside is feeling better. And after I annoyed everybody with my story and faithfully polished my cleaned-up heart every day, I realized my empty heart was longing for purpose. It was then that I looked around and realized Jesus and his disciples needed help. They were schlepping all over the countryside talking, preaching, and healing. They didn't have time to take care of themselves.

Many women were there, watching from a distance. They had followed Jesus from Galilee to care for his needs. —Matt. 27:55

Jesus broke the prevailing custom of his day by including women among his travelling followers. Some were quite wealthy and used their money to support Jesus in his ministry.

He treated his female followers with uncommon dignity and respect.

Well apparently the Holy Spirit gave me the ability to organize, encourage, and serve. I enjoyed doing those things. They didn't seem difficult or stressful to me. So I started using those skills to help Jesus. I found my heartfelt purpose in following and serving him.

I didn't do this by myself. I organized a group of women who had similar abilities. Nobody told us what exactly women who follow Jesus were supposed to do. There were no rules or expectations. There also didn't seem to be any exceptions—everyone was welcome. We chose to follow Jesus, learn from him, and care for him and his disciples. We made sure, whenever Jesus was in Galilee, he and his disciples had food to eat and places to sleep. If their robes needed ironing, we did that. When Jesus and his disciples traveled down to Jerusalem, we often went with him. You know, when you're thankful, nothing seems too hard. And being in Jesus' presence was my joy because I learned so much from him.

I was astonished that Jesus transformed everything broken in me into something useful. I honestly feel that I, the one who was healed, became a healer. All those feelings I had—the isolation, the confusion, the despair, the terrible loneliness—I began recognizing those feelings in others. I could sense the pain in others that was similar to mine, and I *knew* that Jesus' love could help them as well. I didn't need to read the book about it; I understood intuitively. I had an overwhelming sense of Jesus being with me and, as long as I was willing to let him, he continued to heal every broken part of me. I was so grateful.

Even though the name Mary originally meant "bitter," it's become a popular and honored girl's name.

Because of the faithful women who loved and were devoted to Jesus, the name Mary became a symbol of God's grace to women of all times and places.

I guess that change was something I couldn't hide. Other people noticed. The funny thing was, they didn't call me Mary-the-demon-woman. They called me just plain Mary. Because that's who I am.

I am Mary, healed by the gracious act of Jesus my Lord.

I am Mary a willing servant of Jesus choosing to serve with the gifts he gave me.

And as an extra bonus, I finally saw my beautiful city— the city that salted, preserved, and flavored the fish caught in the Sea of Galilee. And I became known as Mary Magdalene. Mary from Magdala. Mary, willing to be salt in a bland and decaying world.

This story can be found in the Gospel of John (20:1–18).

Process and Dig Deeper

1. What did you learn (nutty or valuable as it may be) from the community in which you were raised?

2. Do you know someone whose past has been transformed and whose past makes their present extraordinary?

3. As Mary tells us her story of demon possession, she speaks of being overwhelmed and consumed: Her heart was filled with confusion, fear, despair, sadness, and loneliness. Some theologians say Satan assigns each demon a specific area of temptation with which to bombard people. For example, some demons entice to pride, others to anger, greed, laziness, pride, lust, envy, and gluttony. Others say that one demon can bombard with several temptations. Is it a sin to be tempted? Why or why not?

4. Is it possible to avoid temptation? Do we sometimes set ourselves up to be further tempted? If so, how?

5. Can we resist temptation? What does James mean when he says, "Resist the devil and he will flee from you"? (James 4:7).

6. If we don't resist or flee from the devil, what begins to happen? Or, what happens to our spirit when we habitually surrender to the same temptation day after day?

7. If we repeatedly surrender or succumb to a specific temptation(s), does there come a point where we are overpowered by the demon(s) of that temptation? Explain.

8. Is making a distinction between being *oppressed* by a demon(s) or being *possessed* by a demon(s) helpful? Have you ever experienced oppression or possession of a demon in your life or in the life of someone you know?

9. Have you had the experience of seeing someone released from an overwhelming temptation and eventual victimization that overpowered them for an extended period of time? Describe the process. How does Jesus deliver those he loves from being a victim of demons today?

10. First Corinthians 10:13 says, "No temptation has seized you except what is common to 'man.' And God is faithful; he will not let you be tempted beyond what you can bear. But when you're tempted, he will also provide a way out so that you can stand up under it." What does this verse mean to a twenty-first century woman?

11. What does it mean to be filled with the Holy Spirit? What does it mean that, "Greater is He that is in you than he that is in the world"? (1 John 4:4).

12. According to Galatians 5:22, "the fruit of the Spirit is love, joy, peace, patience, kindness, goodness, faithfulness, gentleness and self-control." What does the Holy Spirit give us if he dwells in our hearts?

13. Ephesians 6:10–18 says, "Finally, be strong in the Lord and in his mighty power. Put on the full armor of God so that you can take your stand against the devil's schemes. For our struggle is not against flesh and blood, but against the rulers, against the authorities, against the powers of this dark world and against the spiritual forces of evil in the heavenly realms.

Therefore put on the full armor of God, so that when the day of evil comes, you may be able to stand your ground, and after you have done everything, to stand. Stand firm then, with the belt of truth . . . the breastplate of righteousness . . . and with your feet fitted with the readiness that comes from the gospel of peace. In addition to all this, take up the shield of faith . . . the helmet of salvation and the sword of the Spirit, which is the word of God." What does it mean to put on the full armor of God?

14. How was Mary's life "salt-like" in its flavoring and preservative powers? What does it mean to be salt in practical terms today? How are you the salt of Jesus today?

5

Mary–Part 2

On Significantly Using the Gifts You're Given

I f I ever dreamed about having a job so important that the world would be changed forever and then wondered what the qualifications would be for that job, I would never have thought being ex-demon-possessed, uneducated, and female would fill the bill. Somehow, I never expected those qualities to top the list.

But that's where Jesus is so alarmingly disarming. When he heals us, he heals inside and out. When he fills us, he fills us way up—his way. When he equips us, he gives us all the tools we need. When he works on a negative in our life, he ends up turning it into a positive. Just so long as we don't doubt that he can really do it.

That's why I love the passionate, thankful, loving, don't-stop-me-from-doing-what-I-love-to-do Mary Magdalene. She didn't spend much time lamenting what she didn't have. That might have stopped her or somehow stymied her. She didn't know her qualifications were meager for a world-changing job. She just responded to the need before her because that is what her eyes of faith and her thankful heart told her to do. She did the job that was obviously before her—at least it was obvious to her—and she did it out of love. I really don't think she even knew it was a job. She never took a "Spiritual Gifts Inventory" to find out what gifts the Holy Spirit gave her. She lived before Pentecost.

I think of a woman I recently met who shows up at her church every Wednesday night for youth group. By looking at her, you would never put her first on the list of people asked to be a youth leader. She doesn't look or act like a youth leader. She wouldn't even call herself a youth leader. But she loves to cook. She knows the kids who show up each week often come hungry. So she prepares meals. And when the kids come into the church kitchen while she's preparing dinner, she asks about their day. They talk to her—really talk. And as she listens, they tell her what they're thinking about, sometimes speaking straight out, sometimes in a way that needs to be read between the lines. They feel safe in her unassuming, love-to-cook presence. So while cooking spaghetti she dispenses grace—just by listening

Mary from Magdala was that type of woman. Because her heart was ready, she responded to the needs in front of her as she came upon them. She saw a need and acted. She didn't ask how, she just did it. And Jesus noticed. Angels noticed. They gave her astounding assignments for which she was uniquely qualified.

I love the drama and the tension in the story as she reveals the weekend of Jesus' death and resurrection. I love the hope she finds in a few words from the transforming Rabboni who called her . . .

Mary

I AM MARY,
>   healed from the isolation and suffering seven
>   demons imposed on me,
>   healed by the gracious love of Jesus my Lord,
>   a willing servant of Jesus choosing to serve with the
>   gifts he gave me.

And that's why when I was at the foot of the cross and saw Jesus completely abandoned by his Father, I recognized that suffering. I heard him cry, "My God, my God, why have you forsaken me?" I understood just a bit what it felt like to be that alone. It tore into the very core of my heart. Into places I thought I had forgotten.

So when that saint of a man, Joseph from Arimathea, offered his tomb as a burial place, I followed him to the cave. My friends and I saw where he laid Jesus' body. We saw him roll the huge stone wheel in front of the opening to the cave.

That was Friday, the beginning of the Sabbath; we Jews have strict laws. Even though I needed burial supplies for Jesus, I would not go to the marketplace on the Sabbath.

Those twenty-four hours my friends and I waited and grieved over what had happened to our Lord.

But as soon as the Sabbath was over at sunset on Saturday night, I gathered spices because I wanted to anoint Jesus' body. We don't embalm bodies, which seems to be a common custom in some cultures. But I wanted to honor Jesus

~

Mary Magdalene went to the disciples with the news: "I have seen the Lord!" And she told them that he had said these things to her. — John 20:18

~

~

According to Jewish law, a criminal's crucified body was not to be left hanging on a tree, but had to be buried the same day. When Jesus died, it was especially important that he was confirmed dead and then buried, because the next day was the Sabbath.

The soldier pierced his side with a sword, confirming his death, but did not crush his bones with a mallet. Numbers 9:12 says that the bones of the Passover Lamb (Jesus) must not be broken.

Nicodemus, a member of the Sanhedrin who had seventy-five pounds of aloe and myrrh at the cross in preparation for burial, was unable to anoint the body of Jesus because of the late hour. No work was to be done on the Sabbath.

~

by putting spices around his body. So early Sunday morning, after hardly sleeping at all and when I couldn't stay in bed any longer, I rounded up my friends.

Jesus' disciples were all holed up in a room. They were sad and, I think, a little scared. But I couldn't stand doing nothing. My friends and I hurried to the tomb, carrying our bags of spices. All of a sudden it dawned on us: How would we move that gigantic stone? Those things weigh a ton and, because they settle into a groove in front of the tomb, they don't roll easily. But you know what? We just went ahead anyway.

Joseph of Arimathea was a member of the Sanhedrin—a group of seventy chief priests, scribes, and elders—who decided to put Jesus to death.

He was a secret disciple who, in offering his tomb for Jesus burial, fulfilled Isaiah 53:9, which says that Jesus was assigned a grave with the rich.

When we got to the tomb, we saw the opening of the cave was already uncovered. The stone was rolled away. I was shocked when I saw that, and frankly, I was scared.

I peeked into the cave. Jesus body wasn't there! It was gone! And if that weren't strange enough, there was a man there who looked like an angel. Sitting in the tomb. I had never seen an angel before. But at this point, I wasn't interested in angels. I just wanted to know where Jesus was. This angel definitely wasn't my Jesus and he didn't seem to have any solid leads about who stole Jesus' body.

All of a sudden, the angel started to talk and told me not to be afraid. Easy for him to say! I don't know what you would do if you saw an angel in the empty tomb where you expected your deceased best friend to be.

I was afraid. The whole scenario was weird.

When the angel told me Jesus wasn't there, I felt like asking him to tell me something I *didn't* know. But then he said, "Jesus is alive." Bizarre. Then he told me to go tell Peter and the other disciples this impossible news. He said I should tell the disciples Jesus would wait for them in Galilee, way up north.

I heard what he said, but I was trying to make sense of the fact that I was chatting with an angel—an angel sitting in the tomb as if he were Jesus' personal assistant, making appointments for him and keeping track of visitors. I was trying to comprehend exactly what he was telling me. Jesus was alive!? He was probably thinking it was okay for a woman to make a fool of herself and spread this outrageous news.

My friends and I did deliver the news to Peter and John. They came running back with us to see what was going on. And then . . . they went back home. Probably to form some sort of committee to figure out what to do next.

But I stayed there, absolutely overcome with grief. Those last days had pierced my heart. Now Jesus' body was gone, I had made appointments for Jesus and his disciples with an angel, and I was left holding a bag of useless spices. I couldn't make sense out of anything. But I didn't have anywhere else to go. And I didn't really want to leave the scene of this crime. So I stayed around to see what would happen next.

~

Knowing Jesus' body had not been anointed, Mary Magdalene brought spices to the tomb, but was unable to anoint his missing body.

Nevertheless, Jesus' body was prepared for burial. Matthew (26:10–11) reports that Jesus tells disciples concerning the woman who poured nard on his head, "Why are you bothering this woman? She has done a beautiful thing to me. . . . When she poured this perfume on my body, she did it to prepare me for burial."

~

When I looked into the tomb again, there were suddenly *two* angels. They questioned me, "Woman, why are you crying?"

It seemed to me these angels were not used to talking to humans. And they asked questions with obvious answers. How could they, of all creatures, not know what had just occurred? I didn't feel like I had time to explain all the details of the last few awful days to ignorant angels, so I cut to the chase, "They have taken my Lord away and I don't know where they have put him."

Then I turned around to leave and saw a man standing there.

He wondered out loud, "Woman, why are you crying? Who is it you are looking for?"

I thought this guy was the gardener and was amazed that he, too, wondered why I was grieving. I replied, "Sir if you have carried him away, tell me where you put him, and I will get him." I assumed he knew I was talking about Jesus' body in the tomb. If this grave was no longer available, I could figure out another way to properly bury Jesus.

Then the man said, "Mary."

"Mary."

I recognized that voice. I turned to him and cried out in Aramaic, the language of my childhood, "Rabboni!"

"Teacher."

I wanted to reach out and hug Jesus. I was so amazed. So confused. The kind of confusion that comes when so many things happen at once. An I-don't-have-time-to-sort-this-all-out confusion.

Then Jesus said, "Do not hold onto me, for I have not yet returned to the Father. Go instead to my brothers and tell them, 'I am returning to my Father, and your Father, to my God and your God.'"

Here I was—Mary, startled out of my wits. And Jesus is asking me—just plain Mary—to get the word out about the most important event in all of history. Of course I didn't quite have such insight that Easter morning But the more I thought and prayed about it, and the more I talked it over with others, that's what I eventually concluded. Me. Mary. A woman. Formerly seven-demon Mary. Healed-by-Jesus Mary.

Thankful-beyond-belief Mary. Jesus trusted *me* with getting the word out about this amazing event, his coming alive after death.

Well, of course I obeyed. I ran to the disciples with the news, "I have seen the Lord!" I told them what Jesus said to me. And they believed me. They didn't call me crazy. It was truly amazing.

I've had some time to look back on that time in my life. And I realize how much grace Jesus lavished on me from the first moment I met him.

List of Spiritual Gifts

Administration
Creative Ability
Discernment
Encouragement
Evangelism
Faith
Giving
Healing
Hospitality
Intercession
Interpretation of Tongues
Knowledge
Leadership
Mercy
Miracles
Prophecy
Service
Shepherding
Speaking in Tongues
Teaching
Wisdom

How he validated me in so many ways as I ministered with him in his ministry.

How he recognized the gifts I didn't even know I had and gave me special opportunities to use them.

How he trusted me as a woman to be the dispenser of the most important news of history.

How he saw my clean and empty heart and filled it with his Spirit.

How he gave me the confidence to see my potential—healed and useful in the kingdom of God.

And most importantly, how he continued to allow me, for the rest of my life, to bring the shadowy spaces of my heart into the light of his presence. The dark and secret places I didn't think mattered to him. He wanted to heal it all, to roll away every one of my stones and heal every last crevice of fear, anger, and self-loathing.

My embarrassments.

My hurts.

The unpleasant people.

The unpleasant experiences.

The circumstances beyond my control.

The ugly deeds done to me.

The ugly words said about me.

The ugly deeds I did.

The ugly words I said.

The mistakes I made.

The decisions I made for good and not-so-good reasons.

The only alternative I had was to tuck all that mess into some dark part of my heart and politely ask Jesus not to become involved. But it seemed to me that when I tried to do that, I started experiencing those feelings of being chained and bound, just as I did when I had the seven demons. And quite frankly I don't know who I thought I was kidding—except myself.

Who knew better than Jesus that there were still broken parts of me?

Who knew better than Jesus that his Spirit could transform those broken parts?

Who knew better than Jesus that by bringing them to his light and dealing with them, I would reflect his glory more and more?

Who knew better than Jesus that he had begun a good work in me, and that he was perfectly capable of completing it?

Who knew better than Jesus that all my vulnerabilities—transformed by the Spirit, forgiven and cleansed by Jesus himself—would give me so much?

The sensitivities to understand his abandonment.
A heart ready to move mountains to minister to him,
even in his death.
And insights that made me uniquely qualified to
serve my Lord, for as long as I lived.

This story can be found in the Gospel of John (20:1–21).

Process and Dig Deeper

1. Identify something you've done that you never thought you were qualified for. What motivated you to do what you did? Were you effective? Have your life experiences changed the focus of what you choose to do or become involved in?

2. Have you ever *not* done something because you were afraid you would fail? What held you back?

3. Who is a person in your life who is a blessing to you? How have they blessed you? Do you think they are aware of how they bless you?

4. Describe Mary Magdalene's personality in this chapter. What do you think contributed to her attitude about life?

5. Mary Magdalene didn't live in Jerusalem. How much energy do you think it took for her to find all the necessary supplies for Jesus' burial in an unfamiliar city?

6. How would you have responded to meeting an angel? Mary seems unimpressed. Why? Who did she really want to see?

7. Have you ever thought about Jesus giving Mary Magdalene the responsibility of being the first person to tell of his resurrection? What might have been some reasons he would choose someone else? Why do you think she was the best candidate to spread the word?

8. Why is it important to think of the Holy Spirit involved in renewing us daily?

9. Where do you sense God isn't finished with you yet?

10. What gifts of the Spirit have you been given? Do you agree that Jesus uses our gifts best out of our brokenness and pain rather than our strengths? If so, why is it that using our gifts out of our brokenness makes them more powerful?

11. Is the Holy Spirit developing gifts in you? Are you surprised? Excited? Hesitant? Are you ready to go for it? Why or why not?

6

Finished Its

On Forgiveness

P ronouns are inconclusive words unless we know what noun they are attached to. When I taught seventh grade, my students regularly saw circles around pronouns begging for an antecedent. Sentences change when the pronoun is misinterpreted.

Imagine the variety of images that could come to mind if I wrote to my mother, "Glenn told me Matt stepped on his finger and broke it while they were mowing the neighbor's lawn." My mother may have been led to believe that Matt stepped on his own finger, when actually Matt stepped on Glenn's finger. (Don't even ask!) But because the pronouns "he" and "his" are unclear, you could never be sure whose finger was stepped on.

How many times have I heard Jesus' words on the cross? Probably every Good Friday since I have been cognizant of Good Friday. The seven sayings of the cross are familiar to me. I know them. They touch me. I know immediately as the reading begins, and the sanctuary becomes dark, that when the last candle of the seventh word is extinguished, I'll feel sad. Very sad. I know I'll sing, "Were you there when they crucified my Lord?" and feel a knot in my stomach and a tightening in my throat. That is part of my Good Friday experience.

That is why I surely didn't expect to feel analytical one Good Friday when I heard, "It is finished." I didn't expect to feel frustrated. I was embarrassed that my first feeling was to put a mental circle around "it." I wanted to send it back to Jesus on the cross and ask him to clarify which noun he was referencing.

And what did "finished" mean? We finish unloading the dishwasher. But sure as our family eats, there will be another load of dirty dishes the next day. Is it finished forever or just until the next time?

Was my friend who died at such a young age finished? Is my ninety-five-year-old father-in-law, who does not recognize my husband, unfinished? Was my daughter finished with her foot when she fell from a ladder and two years later needed to have that same foot amputated? Are shooting victims finished with a fulfilled life when they are paralyzed from the waist down? Are we ever finished making unwise decisions? Can a child, because of birth, gender, nationality, or status, ever finish the negative stigma which society often places on them? Can someone who has become accustomed to living off the backs and hard work of others ever finish thinking they deserve everything they get?

When is an artist finished with a masterpiece? When is a mother's influence on her child finished? When is a lesson plan finished?

When is the remodel job finished? The electrician leaves and says "it" is finished. Then the plumber walks in, works for a few days, and leaves saying "it" is finished. The dry wall and painting has to be done next, and when those workers leave, they say "it" is finished. And yet there is always one more "it" that needs finishing. Many "its" were finished and yet "it" wasn't finished.

The year my church sanctuary was dark and "Were You There?" was sung, I found myself questioning Jesus, and none too patiently. What was "it"? And how finished was "finished"?

So I stand near the faithful women who loved Jesus. Women who ministered to him and followed him. Women whose lives were changed by him. His mother, his aunt, and many others.

But I stand at a distance because I wonder.

I wonder if he really loves me.

I wonder if he knows all my "its."

I wonder if he can really finish all those "its."

And I ask a suffering Jesus if he can clarify.

Finished "Its"

IF I WERE ONE OF THE WOMEN standing at the foot of the cross on Good Friday afternoon, I would have fixated on the despair of the moment. I would have felt the passion and horror of what was happening in front of my eyes. I know that.

> *When he had received the drink, Jesus said, "It is finished." With that, he bowed his head and gave up his spirit. —John 19:30*

I know I would have felt the sadness Jesus' mother wore like a cloak. I know I would have been frightened by the anger of Jesus' accusers, and I would have felt helpless and powerless to stop the abuse. I know I would have been stunned by the hatred, hurt by the demeaning actions of the soldiers, and repulsed by so many people's cruelty.

And I know I would have been awed by the intensity of the few words Jesus spoke, conceived in pain yet born in love.

I don't know if you have experienced what I'm about to describe. Sometimes little things can pop up in the most poignant moments of life and send you off into another place in your head. They interrupt a tragic event, stroll into a tearful confession, and distract us during a passionate conversation.

It's embarrassing to admit, but if I had been one of the faithful women standing at the foot of the cross when Jesus cried "It is finished," I might have missed the gravity of what was happening. I might have had one of those moments when I get sidetracked. In my fractured thinking, I might have wondered what in the world Jesus meant when he said, "It is finished."

Jesus' seven words on the cross:

"Father forgive them, for they know not what they do."

"Today you will be with me in paradise."

"Behold your son: behold your mother."

"My God, my God, why have you forsaken me?"

"I thirst."

"It is finished."

"Father, into your hands I commit my spirit."

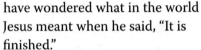

At first hearing, I may have thought Jesus was saying, "Finally. The humiliation I endured for thirty-three years is finished. The rejection, the being misunderstood, the fatigue, the living without a permanent place to call my home, the endless hours of teaching, preaching, and healing—it is all finished. The last several days of a wild crowd hailing me, the suffering in the garden, the miles of walking to and from the Garden of Gethsemane. Being hauled before a judicial system and being completely misrepresented. The beatings, the torture, and the long walk with a heavy cross. The nails being driven into my body, the crown of thorns, the shouting crowds condemning me, and the sorrow on my mother's face. The hate. All the hate . . . it is all finished. It's done. No more."

I might have walked away from the foot of the cross with this understanding of "It is finished" and felt very grateful for all Jesus did. What a hero. What a suffering servant. How glad I was to have known him. How happy I was to be loved by him.

But if I were persistent, that "it" might keep nagging at me and become a lot more difficult to deal with. At least if I were being honest. When Jesus hung on that cross and spoke those words, and finally came to "It is finished," he wasn't looking at himself and thinking about his own torturous experiences; he had me in his mind's eye. Me.

If he had any strength left, he might have said, "Take some time to ponder what the 'it' is. Sit quietly and think:

The 'its' are not mine. They are yours.
All of your 'its' indict you as guilty before the holy God of heaven and earth.
All of your 'its' keep you from living freely right now.
All the times you heard what I told you, listened to my words, thought about them, realized how important they were, and then turned and did not allow them to penetrate your living; all of those became your 'its.'
And I finished them for you."

If I were one of the women at the foot of the cross, and was willing to be really honest, I might have begun an "Its" List. If I didn't get distracted, the following might be on my list.

Every arrogance I show.

Every time I whine and don't see God's gifts to me.

Every deceit.

Every jealousy.

Every time I cover up a sin instead of admitting it.

Every excuse I make to defend a sinful attitude.

Every time my anger boils up and explodes.

Every time I let my anger simmer.

Every time I see the splinter in another's eye and miss the two-by-four in my own.

Every time I piously bury my junk, thinking I can get rid of it that way.

Every greedy act.

Every insensitive remark or snide comment.

Every "poor me" attitude.

Every bitterness.

Every remembering and holding onto old hurts.

Every time I compare myself to someone else and feel superior.

Every time I compare myself to someone else and feel inferior.

Every time I defend that attitude by being annoying.

Every time I pretend to be nicer than I really am, hoping for some kind of payoff.

Every time I take something that doesn't belong to me.

Every time I refuse to forgive.

Every time I blame somebody else instead of taking my own responsibility.

Every time I tolerate sinful behavior in my home or in my life because it's just too hard to deal with.

Every time I manipulate situations so that I can be in control.

Every time I manipulate those around me to serve my own needs.

Every time I interrupt and don't listen.

Every time I'm the one with the answer to everybody's problem.

Every time I'm selfish and do nothing when someone needs my help.

Every time I help because I think I know how to solve every problem.

Every time I put myself on the throne of my life (tiara and all) instead of the Holy One who belongs there.

Every unexamined blind spot.

Those would be some of my "its." There are more. And each "it" shows me heavily in debt to the justice of the God of heaven and earth.

But I have a tendency to ask for forgiveness for some of those sins, and then go on and continue in them. I find it hard to change old patterns of behavior. It's difficult to admit to some attitude I've lived with all my life and then change it. I'd rather just be thankful Jesus died for that stuff. I'm delighted he forgives me. I like being forgiven of the guilt of my sins, but I'm not so sure I have the energy to finish them.

When Jesus said, "It is finished," he was saying, "I recognized your debt, and because I love you:

I paid the full price for all your nouns.
I erased every 'it' you don't even pay attention to.
I wiped out every sin you tend to overlook.
I unmasked every hurt you try so hard to cover up.
I separated all of your 'its' as far as the east is from west.
I stamped 'paid in full' over all your 'its.'
All your 'its' are healed.
All your nouns are forgiven.
And now, I wonder if you can gratefully accept
It is finished."

And each time you're tempted to return to the "nouns" that don't allow you to live in freedom, remember I am willing to finish them.

Through the power of my Spirit, you can turn away from any "it" and choose a healthier response.

If I were one of the women at the foot of the cross, I would have treasured such words spoken by my Jesus. And then, if I had seen the empty tomb on Easter morning, I would have realized that Jesus demonstrated—with all the power of heaven and earth, of the alpha and omega, and the heavenly heights—that whatever "it" is, "It is finished." I'm fully forgiven. I'm completely free.

Now, if only I could accept the gift by thoroughly forgiving myself. That would be heaven on earth.

This story can be found in the Gospel of John (19:28–30).

Process and Dig Deeper

1. What were your personal or family Good Friday traditions when you were a child? What feelings were evoked?

2. Describe something that is completely finished in your life. Can something be finished yet still unfinished? Is there something personal in your life that you thought seemed finished, but later you discovered it wasn't finished?

3. If you had been at the cross, where would you have stood? Close? With others? Alone? A ways away?

4. Are there other "its" we could consider finished? What about past hurts done to us by others? Do they fall into the "it" category? What about sins we were involved in before we knew they were wrong?

5. Is it difficult to accept *total* forgiveness and acceptance from God the Father through Jesus?

6. Is it possible to accept forgiveness from the guilt of our sins and still feel ashamed? What does it take to feel fully accepted?

7. If we feel shame for past hurts and sins, does such shame drive us to act in particular ways? What actions—observed in yourself or in others—speak loudly that total forgiveness hasn't been accepted?

8. The disciple Peter denied Jesus three times and then fell asleep when Jesus needed him. Yet on Pentecost morning, he

preached with passion and power saying, "The promise is for you and your children and for all that are far off. . . ." What do you hope your children (nieces, nephews, grandchildren) in today's culture will receive from Good Friday's "It is Finished" word on the cross?

9. Can you tell that you respond differently, act differently, or think differently about something that used to get you down because of the finishing work of Jesus on the cross? Tell someone how you have personally experienced the truth of Jesus' words, "It is finished."

7

D-List People on Jesus' A-List

On the Heart of True ~~Religion~~ Worship

Funny how, in Jesus' world, everything seems to be turned inside out and upside down. It's the kind of world where— if I watch and listen with my heart—as soon as I have something figured out, I know I don't have much figured out. How is it that in Jesus' world the poor are rich and the weak are strong? The humble are great and the great are humbled? The last are first and the first are last? How is it that the needy are privileged while the privileged are needy? Those who know the most lack understanding, and those who supposedly know the least nevertheless understand some of the deepest matters of the heart?

Jesus didn't go to the most theologically worthy seminaries to find his twelve disciples. How is it that Jesus chose a guy who ripped off good people through exorbitant taxes to be one of his treasured disciples? How is it that he chose an impulsive hothead to be the one on whom he built his church? How is it that he chose a guy with anger-management problems to be the apostle of love? How is it he chose to enlist a woman with a more-than-questionable past to become one of the first evangelists?

Why is it I found rich measures of Jesus' lavish grace and wisdom in a smoke-filled Al Anon meeting, as I sat with worried, anxious, and angry family members who were learning to release? Release the one they loved who was determined to destroy themselves by abusing drugs or alcohol? We were learning the delicate balance of release but not rejecting that very person who was so self-destructive and creating chaos in the whole extended family. It was from them I learned I had no business—from my own moral superiority—trying to control or "fix" those who have given up on themselves. Rather, I needed to learn what unconditional love really means—a lifelong lesson I'm still trying to wrap my brain around and take to heart.

Why is it that a man in Ecuador, who owned nothing except maybe the chicken under his house—a man who had never heard the good news about Jesus—not only cooked his only chicken for my husband's dinner, but also gifted him with a lovely handmade piece of pottery? Just because.

Why is it I felt like I had just taken a shower of grace at my very first writers' critique meeting as I talked with people who, at that time, were strangers? They read a very flawed manuscript written by me, an inexperienced author. They didn't say the manuscript was bad; they didn't say it was good. They were not patronizing, making me feel like when I grow up I might be good at this, but instead they said, "What suggestions can we make so Ruth can get this published?" And it eventually was.

Why is it I so often judge someone on how they come across, or what they look like, or how they are dressed, rather than taking a couple of seconds to look below the surface and see them through the eyes of Jesus? Why is it that I know this, I espouse this, I think it is the right thing to do, and yet my heart is hardened enough to judge first rather than to be gracious? Why is it I place my own values first and consequently other people's as less valuable?

In about thirty verses of scripture, I meet Jesus nudging a woman into seeing herself as valuable. Years ago she gave up on anyone treating her graciously. Yet Jesus saw possibilities and potential in her. He knew she was created in his image. He reassures the woman and us that he would rather do his good work on our inside rather than on our outside—in spite of the fact that we usually concentrate on *looking* good to others rather than *being* good to ourselves and others. He looks within us and sees hope, whereas we look at our projected image and see unfixable flaws. When he asks his quiet, qualitative, quintessential questions, his grace breaks in.

In an encounter with Jesus at a Samaritan well, the woman responds to his probing questions. She gathers everyone she knows to join her in meeting someone who is willing to talk to her openly, honestly, and engagingly. A person who knows her serious issues yet respects her.

When I hear this woman's story, I realize I'm meeting someone who encounters the lavish grace of Jesus, and she becomes . . .

A D-List Woman on Jesus' A-List

I DIDN'T TRY TO LIVE MY LIFE so that I became an easy target for the wagging tongues of the town of Sychar. Stuff just happened. One poor decision followed by another. But I'm a survivor. I have my own friends. We're not on Sychar, Samaria's A-list of Who's Who. As a matter of fact, we're probably at the bottom of the D-list. You'd be more likely to find us at some "Whatever Anonymous" meeting than at fancy social gatherings.

To prevent a lot of hassles for myself, I go to the well for water at noon. Some might say I should have my head examined for taking care of this task at the hottest time of the day. Especially at my age. And let me tell you, more than once I questioned my own sanity. Lugging pots full of water through the stifling heat isn't fun.

But I wasn't born yesterday. The few times I went to the well early in the morning, the young girls whispered to each other and avoided eye contact with me. I may have messed up my life, but I'm not stupid. I knew by their glances that I was the woman their mothers had warned them about. "Don't act like her. Don't make the same irresponsible decisions she made. You be careful now; you don't want her reputation." And so on and so on.

Then, leaving her water jar, the woman went back to the town and said to the people,

"Come, see a man who told me everything I ever did. Could this be the Christ?"
—John 4:28, 29

So after a while it was just a lot easier for them, and for me, if I went to get water at noon. Oh well.

One day as I walked up to the well, a man, who might be a teacher was listening to his friends griping about having to travel through our Samaritan village.

Didn't he know Jews and Samaritans don't get along with each other?

And they would have preferred to go the long way to Galilee from Jerusalem rather than take this shortcut through Samaria.

And they were out of food.

And it was hot.

And where would they go to get lunch?

And how were they going to get water out of the well without a bucket?

Eventually they must have gotten tired of whining and went into town to buy some lunch. I just pretended I hadn't

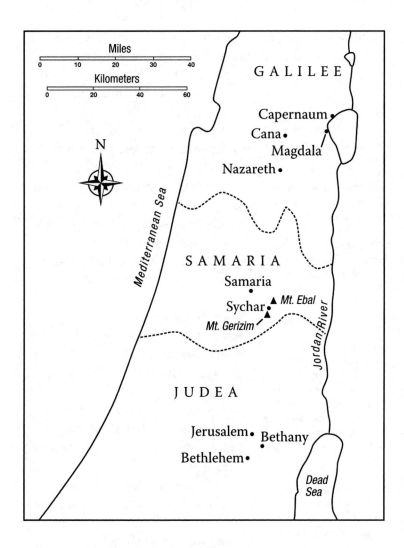

noticed anything and got ready to fill my water pots. Then suddenly the quiet teacher who had stayed behind asked me, "Will you give me a drink of water?"

As I said, I wasn't born yesterday. I wasn't going to let this guy take advantage of me. He could get away with asking me for water because he's a man. Not only that, he's a Jew. But that was about all I was going to let him say to me. I just wanted to get water and get home before others showed up.

Jews and Samaritans had long hated each other.

Ancestry
At the end of the era of the kings and prophets of Israel, many Jews were removed from central Palestine (Samaria) and taken to Babylon. Pagan neighbors moved in and intermarried with some of the resident Jews. The Jews despised these people, considering them half-breeds.

Religion
The Jews lived by all the books of the Old Testament. The Samaritans lived by their own version of the Torah—the Samaritan Pentateuch—which included only the five books of Moses and was said to be older than the Jewish copy of the Torah.

Samaritans traced their ancestry to the northern Kingdom of Israel. They claimed to be more closely related to Abraham than the Jews who lived in Judea and Galilee.

And so the rival Samaritans and the Jews taunted each other viciously.

After all, I'm a Samaritan woman, stuck in this town and carrying my lousy reputation. If word got out I talked to this Jewish guy and even gave him water, the self-righteous girls would feast over the gossip that night. My reputation would be even further shot. I didn't need the added grief.

So I didn't look at him. I didn't even want to appear friendly in case somebody walked by. I just went about my business. But he kept looking my way without getting his own water, so I finally said, "Why are you asking me, of all people, for water?"

Instead of answering my question, he told me that if I would ask him for living water he would give me some.

Right! A clueless Jewish guy without a water pot, who asked me for a drink, was now offering me living water! Good grief!

I looked at him squarely in the eyes to make sure he wasn't hallucinating. Then I took one small step toward him, put my hands on my hips, and said, "Excuse me, Sir.

You don't have a bucket. So you can't possibly get water out of this well, which, you probably don't know, was originally owned by my own ancestor, Jacob."

I hope you realize how fast I had to think in this situation. I knew men like him that always hold all the cards. I thought I'd let him know that even though I knew he would call Jacob *his* ancestor, I also called Jacob *my* ancestor. He was on my ground, too. I didn't want to start an argument, but I figured he'd better know not to mess with me. I was proud of myself.

Then this clown without a water pot told me that if he gave me water, I would never be thirsty again. Can you believe it? In fact, he said I would have an internal, eternal spring inside of me. This sounded pretty crazy to me, but I went along with it anyway—just for the fun.

∼

Jesus met the woman in Sychar, Samaria at Jacob's well.

Just before dying, Jacob gave his son Joseph this land (Gen. 48:21–22). Water was vital for survival and well-being in the ancient Near East, so this gift of land with a viable well was important.

It is significant that Jesus speaks to this Samaritan woman—hated by the Jews—about the importance of living water at a well that was given by one of the patriarchs of the Jewish faith.

∼

"Do you mean that if I take your water, I won't get thirsty and I won't have to come back to this well anymore?" "Impossible," I thought to myself—but if it were true it sure would make my life a little bit easier.

Instead of answering, he pulled a fast one on me. He said, "Go get your husband and come back and talk to me."

I don't know why he thought he had to talk to my husband. In fact, I thought he was getting unnecessarily nosy. On the other hand, if he was new in town, I figured he wouldn't have looked up my marriage records. But I told him straight out, "I don't have a husband."

He said, "You just told the truth. You don't have a husband. In fact you have had five husbands and you are not married to the man you are now living with."

I'm used to people talking about me behind my back. But I never expected somebody—especially a despised outsider—to just come out and tell me what was wrong with me. On the other hand, I didn't feel like discussing this with him, so I replied, "Oh, so you must be a prophet."

Then, as long as he was getting personal, I thought I'd poke at *him* a little. Get the subject off myself and onto him. "You know, our fathers worshiped on this mountain, but you Jews claim that the place where we must worship is in Jerusalem."

He didn't take the bait. He quickly added, "Soon it won't matter where you worship."

"Oh, really now," I snapped back at him. "And is that why you Jews make such a big deal about going to the temple in Jerusalem?"

He just went on. Quietly. Like nothing I could say would fluster him. "It won't matter where you worship. The only thing that will matter is whether you worship truthfully and with a ready and willing spirit."

I didn't get what he was talking about, so I concluded, "Well, never mind. Pretty soon there's going to be a Messiah and when he comes, he'll explain everything to me for real."

Then he dropped a bombshell on me. "I'm the Messiah," he said.

I'm sure my mouth fell down to my knees. Why in the world would some thirsty prophet from Galilee with a ragtag group of griping followers, hanging out at a well without a water pot, even claim to be the Messiah? And if he were the Messiah, why was he sitting at my well at noon asking me for water? And if he really were the Messiah, why would he tell *me* about it? Why wouldn't he go to the temple in

Jerusalem and announce it to all the supposedly important people there? Why wouldn't he tell a man this information? Why wouldn't he inform those guys he was with? If he were going to tell a woman, why me? And how did he know all about me? And if he knew all this stuff about me, why was he being so nice to me? The whole scene was just too comical to believe.

Besides, I didn't know if I could trust somebody this kind. But I saw his friends coming back with lunch and I was sure our conversation was over. They looked at their friend, and then at me, and then back at their friend. They didn't say anything, but busily laid out their lunch.

I decided to put down my water pots. I didn't want to take the time to fill them. I didn't want to be dragged down carrying them back to town full of water.

While the man and his friends ate their lunch, I ran into town and found all my friends. I said, "You better come to the well with me. There's a guy there who knows all about me. And he talked to me even though I didn't lead him on. Really. And he was nice to me. And he told me mysteries that made some sense to me. He says he's the Messiah. Maybe so. So come with me, and you can check him out yourselves."

My friends dropped everything and ran with me. When they saw this man, whose name I found out was Jesus, they listened to him. And they had the same impression I did. He seemed authentic.

My friends chatted among themselves. "This man does make some sense. Just like she said."

"This must be the Messiah we've been waiting for. Who else could he be?"

"He speaks with real authority."

Then, wonder of wonders, my friends began saying things like, "We do believe you are the Messiah."

"You are the one we have been longing for."

"If our friend says you are the one who we have been waiting for, then we also believe."

Their confidence warmed my heart. Not too many people listened to me about anything. And now, because we believed him, this Jesus stayed in our town for two days. More and more of my D-list friends came and listened to him talk. And when they heard him, they knew Jesus was the Messiah. It was a stunning series of events at that well.

The man's friends looked a bit bewildered, like they themselves had no idea what was going on. They truly seemed baffled. Samaritans? Jews? Jesus? A woman? D-list people? Ironically, these guys that hung out with this Messiah couldn't put it all together any better than I could.

Yet we all—Jews and Samaritans, male and female—had gathered together at Jacob's well.

Receiving water from a man without a water pot.

Drawing from a well of living water, creating an internal, eternal spring in each of us who recognized him as the promised Messiah.

The Samaritans who gathered with me were D-list people, suddenly welcomed onto Jesus' A-list.

This story can be found in the Gospel of John (4:1–42).

Process and Dig Deeper

1. What does it say to you about Jesus' values when the strong are weak (2 Corinthians 12:9); the last are first (Matthew 19:30); and the poor are rich? (2 Corinthians 6:10, 8:9).

2. How would you describe the Samaritan woman to someone? How old was she? Was she pretty? What was her body language? Her vocal volume and tone?

3. Why do you think the disciples were so uncomfortable about going through Samaria?

4. Why are we so hesitant to settle old differences? What prohibits us from doing it? What are the results when we do?

5. Why do you think Jesus revealed so much about himself to the Samaritan woman? What happened as a result of him talking with her?

6. Do you ever feel like a "Samaritan"? Because of your gender? Race? Nationality? Marital status? Past mistakes? Job? Do you think that feeling could ever be changed by Jesus?

7. Is the "D-list" a reality in our lives today? How have you seen it expressed? Have you ever been on it?

8. Do you remember a time when you were blessed in an unexpected place, at an unexpected time, from an unexpected person?

9. What does the Apostle Paul mean when he says, "God is no respecter of persons"? (Acts 10:34 KJV).

10. Do you think the Samaritan woman continued going to the well at noon after her encounter with Jesus? If not, what time do you think she went? Why? What might cause her to change her ways?

11. When Jesus spoke to the woman at the well, he said true worshippers would worship in spirit and in truth (John 4:24). What is a true worshiper?

12. Does the Samaritan woman's story connect with your story in any way? How is she like you? How is she different from you?

8

Longing For a Miracle

On the Source of Healing

A few weeks ago, I met with a group of friends and threw out the question, "What do you long for?" It was surprising how difficult that question was to answer. One woman would throw out a longing and then say, "No, that's not it." Another would throw out a suggestion and then say, "No, that's not it." We came to the conclusion that perhaps we as women hardly know what we long for. So we all promised each other we would go home, think about this, and when we met again, we'd share our conclusions.

Well, I did that, and I came to the conclusion that I'm a woman who often longs for the way things could be. When I was a little girl, I poured over the pictures of Adam and Eve in my children's Bible. You probably know the ones: Adam and Eve in Paradise, working together, taking care of the beasts and tending a weedless garden. I think I've carried those pictures into my adult life. Maybe the little girl inside of me is still longing for the normal in my life to be a little more like the normal of Adam and Eve's Paradise . . . except with clothes on.

I long to be loved.

I long for healthy, significant relationships. Relationships with mutual respect.

I long to have a clear awareness of my purpose in life.

I long for our warring world to be peaceful.

I long for the bitter to be sweet.

For the disenfranchised to feel valued.

For the worried to find release.

For the shamed and guilty to know forgiveness.

For the hungry to be full.

For the sick to be healed.

For the broken to become whole.

For the angry to be free.

For the confused to gain clarity.

For the sad to feel happy.

When I was interviewing the person who inspired the main character of my children's book *Always With You*, I was amazed at the miraculous ways Jesus works to meet our longings when we are least aware of it. That story is about Kim, a four-year-old girl who was the lone survivor in her Vietnam village after a Viet Cong attack. As Kim's mother lay dying, she whispered three sentences: "Come to me." "Don't be afraid." "I will always be with you." Those are Jesus' words, spoken by a mother who probably never knew him. Yet those words carried Kim through terror, displacement, physical difficulties, loss of family, and a host of other griefs and longings a child should never have to endure and which left scars in her heart. When she met Jesus through the work of Christian missionaries, however, she realized that her mother's words were Jesus' words to her. She realized Jesus was already providing for healing of her pain long before she ever knew him.

When I realize that Jesus cares—really cares—about my heart's deepest longings, I take a leap of faith and no longer imagine what it was like to be one of the women whose lives intersected with Jesus. I *become* one of those women. Knowing that he alone can fulfill my longings, I follow Jesus through the Gospels, watching his every move and bearing witness to the miracles he performs. I hear him say, "Come to me." "Don't be afraid." "I will always be with you."

I walk with him as he touches lives in ways I could never imagine. And I see myself as a woman who is, even in the twenty-first century . . .

Bearing Witness to a Miracle–My Miracle

IN THIS LAST CHAPTER, I, Ruth, am one of the women in the crowd who follows Jesus as he walks through the Gospels. I have the privilege of seeing him at the beginning of his ministry. I'm excited to follow a leader who is:

so fresh,
so filled with integrity and a healthy authority,
so able to do the unimaginable,
so compassionate,
so wise,
so visionary,
so willing to teach truths about a new order of living
he calls the kingdom of God,
so able to communicate the heart of God,
and so hopeful.

I have hope that this man is more than able to create and sustain the sweet existence I long for. And as I witness first-hand Jesus' many miracles, I'm filled with hope that maybe, just maybe, in the right place and at the right time, Jesus will see me; he will reach out to me, and say, "I want to make the normal of your life a little more like the normal of Paradise."

But when I see him perform his first miracle, I wonder what he is thinking. For his first miracle, he chooses to transform 120 gallons of water into 120 gallons of wine. And he does this at the *end* of the wedding. After everyone already

John 2:6 says, "Nearby stood six stone water jars, the kind used by the Jews for ceremonial (ritual) washing, each holding from twenty to thirty gallons."

Mark 7:3–4 says, "The Pharisees and all the Jews do not eat unless they give their hands a ceremonial washing, holding to the tradition of the elders. When they come from the marketplace they do not eat unless they wash. And they observe many other traditions, such as the washing of cups, pitchers, and kettles."

Cleansing was an important spiritual exercise in the Jewish religion. Originally, God instituted these purification laws. He instructed Moses to teach the Jewish people to observe them. Later the Pharisees added more cleansing laws. These laws became an obsession.

One-sixth of the Jewish Talmud—an extensive record of rabbinic discussions about Jewish law, customs, and history—is about washings and cleansings.

had plenty to drink. Using the 120 gallons of water intended for a ritual washing that would let everybody know they were clean before God. And filling the pots which stood ready for the wedding guests to ceremonially cleanse themselves from the defilement of their everyday living.

Those pots. That water. Miraculously transformed into the finest wine served at the wedding. Why?

And then as I follow him, I wonder why someone as compassionate as Jesus passes by so many lepers and heals only a few. Yet when he does choose to heal a particular leper, he doesn't just stand in front of the man saying, "Be clean." Instead, Jesus defiles himself. He kneels down and touches the leper and says, "Be clean."

I like that, But, why does he do it?

I wonder why Jesus sleeps through a wild storm in the bottom of a boat. A boat on the verge of breaking apart. And then when he's awakened, he stands up in that boat, with his terrified disciples accusing him of not caring if they drown, and calmly addresses the wind and the waves, "Quiet. Be still."

Why?

As I walk with him, I wonder why, when Jesus frees people from the tyranny of demon possession, he speaks directly to the demons and not only demands that they be quiet, but also banishes them.

Why was that important?

I wonder how, at the end of a busy day of teaching, he has the energy and creativity to feed five thousand hungry people. He could have sent them away to the nearby towns and told them to buy their own food. But instead, he takes the offering of a small boy—five loaves and two fishes—and feeds everyone. And, as his disciples notice, he still has twelve baskets of leftovers.

Why?

Why does he heal the daughter of a woman who lives *outside* of Israel—a Gentile from Syrophoenicia. A woman who knows she is seen as a dog begging for crumbs from the table of the Jews. Why her little girl, and not little girls in his own country?

Why does he heal a woman—bent over for eighteen years from a debilitating condition—on the Sabbath, in the synagogue, right in front of his worst critics?

Why does he heal one deaf man and then, a bit later, a man who is blind?

Why them? Why not everyone? Why not every child? Why not wholesale healing of every sick and wounded person in the world? Wouldn't that be nice?

Why are there only thirty-five recorded miracles in his entire ministry? And why are only twenty of those miracles healings or raising people back to life? Why didn't Jesus make the normal of Paradise the normal for everyone? He could have.

So I wonder, why did Jesus perform miracles at all? Did some lucky people just happen to be in his way on a good day when he felt like healing? He could have spent all his time healing. Did Jesus have some kind of a quota system—or particular requirements?

Then I wonder if I have misunderstood Jesus' miracles and what he intended by them. Have I fantasized about his miracles in much the way I fantasize about the way things could be?

It's interesting and so helpful to recognize that John, the beloved apostle, probably anticipated questions like mine. And he addressed them right after he told the story of the wedding in Cana. He said, "This was the first of his miraculous signs . . . [Jesus] thus revealed his glory" (John 2:11).

Hmmm. Water to wine, a sign? A sign tells me something. It reveals something. A sign points me to a new reality or in a new direction. So *what* were these signs telling me? John helps me with this also. By using the word "sign," he tells me that the actual miracle wasn't as important as what it signified. Those miracles revealed Jesus' glory. The real Jesus. Who he was. What he was really all about.

After Jesus turns the water to wine, the apostle John says, "This, the first of his miraculous signs, Jesus performed in Cana of Galilee. He thus revealed his glory, and his disciples put their faith in him" (John 2:11).

Those signs give me a hint about the kind of kingdom Jesus came to establish. A new social order he was trying to create. A new way of living in community. This wasn't an artificial theme park kind of kingdom. Not a put-on-the-costume, paint-on-a-happy-face-for-as-long-as-you-are-on-the-clock kind of kingdom. The members of this kingdom would not have a take-time-off-and-then-come-back-and-do-it-again-the-next-day personality.

Jesus' signs tell me what was important to him. The signs tell me he was establishing a new, 24/7, all-encompassing, even miraculous kind of reality. An authentic, beautiful, fresh, loving, and kind kingdom. Where people would be healthy in soul, body, mind, and emotion.

Jesus' signs help me see how he related to women in a radical, revolutionary way, especially compared to his culture's norms. They reveal how he turned his world upside down as he valued and interacted with *all* types of people.

And Jesus' signs also hint at my own place in his kingdom. I'm a part of this kingdom, with an imperfect reality in the here and now, but with a perfect reality coming in the future. I'm a significant person in this kingdom. I'm precious to Jesus. He loves me. And in this kingdom—where its Lord calls himself the Way, and the Truth, and the Life—Jesus is also *my* Way, *my* Truth, and *my* Life.

Jesus is my healer. My miracle worker. And his signs are for me. Not just for my brother or my sister, but for me. In that light, I look at these signs of Jesus again. And they become personal. For me. They become mine as well as his.

John the Baptist sent his personal disciples to ask Jesus, "Are you the one who was to come, or should we expect someone else?" Jesus replied, "Go back and report to John what you hear and see: the blind receive sight, the lame walk, those who have leprosy are cured, the deaf hear. . . ." (Matt. 11:3–5).

At the wedding, when Jesus transforms the water in those ceremonial washing pots into wine, he makes a bold, controversial statement. His actions show what he thinks about anyone trying to prove their love for God with a long list of "dos" and "don'ts" or meaningless ceremonies and rituals. He turns water into wine to illustrate that the kingdom of God is a celebration—even a party.

A party? Yes. Not a mere ritual. A party of relationship with him. And for me, it's a relationship where all I have to do is gratefully celebrate his amazing love. He's saying—without uttering a word—that in his kingdom it's okay for my heart to be glad and for me to have a free spirit. He's suggesting that it might be good for me to take a look at my life and uncover what I do to try to get others to love me. What I do to play God in my own life and the lives of those around me. What I do to prove to those around me that I'm a really good person worthy of their attention and affection. Jesus reminds me that all these things end up tying a noose around my neck. They prevent me from living joyfully in peace and freedom. They don't come from a heart of peace and joy and freedom, but from a heart bound by approval-seeking. In his first miracle, Jesus is inviting me to a kingdom party. Right now. The invitations are in everyone's own mailbox, awaiting an RSVP.

What about that healed leper? With this sign, Jesus points me to a new age where two things will happen. First, I'll never be so untouchable that I should be ostracized. There is nothing I have thought or done which is so bad that Jesus will not care about and for me. But this sign also shows me, ironically, that I—who often considers myself fairly spotless—have leprous corners of my heart which Jesus can see. And in spite of that, he stoops down to me, touches me, cleans me inside and out, and then tells me to go back where I live and testify that he has worked a miracle in my life. I didn't do it by myself; he made himself unclean, touched me, and now I'm whole.

And then there is the storm, and the boat, and the frightened disciples—a picture of Jesus calming the storms in my life.

Even when I stand in my little boat and ask him if he really cares.

Even when I shake my finger at him and ask in accusatory tones why he isn't moving faster to calm my storms. Even when I'm most desperate.

He settles my stormy life. He quiets my personal storm's fury so I can be quiet in my heart.

And if the healing from demons is a sign, then it has to be a sign for me to recognize, admit, and confess the attitudes that are suffocating my spirit. And it must be a sign for me to call on the name of Jesus. For there is power in his name—even the demons didn't dare to say it—and he is more than able to speak directly to, to quiet, and to remove the fears, worries, anxieties, and addictions which plague me.

Feeding five thousand people with five loaves and two fish is another personal sign for me. It reminds me that if Jesus can take the few resources of a little boy and multiply their effect, then he can certainly use my few talents. He miraculously tends to so many of my needs. And just as Jesus provided miraculously for thousands from the gift of a little boy who naively believed his meager resources could fix the problem, he also sees me as a child who has something of value with which I can bless many.

This chorus got me through my child-rearing years:

I cast all my cares upon You,
I lay all of my burdens down at Your feet.
And any time I don't know what to do,
I will cast all my cares upon You.

—Kelly Willard, "I Cast All My Cares Upon You"

Then there's the woman who knows she doesn't belong in the crowd in which she's found herself. Yet she asks Jesus for a miracle in front of those who cherish their exclusiveness, begging only for a few table crumbs. And when I see Jesus heal her little girl, I see the compassionate, generous spirit of Jesus. He includes her. And when I see that, I know he compassionately steps into my life, too. And he offers me way more than a few crumbs for becoming lavishly loved in his kingdom.

Jesus heals the bent-over woman and helps her stand straight again. A sign—a picture to me—that he can set me free from the load I feel compelled to sling over my shoulder. He can relieve my spine, curved with all the burdens I carry, the events and people I seek to control, and the rules I follow in order to call myself right and pure. He can heal me of my own addiction to all the rules which are so far from the grace of God. The same suffocating rules which morph based on where I am, who I'm with, and what community I happen to be living in. He's telling me, "Stand up straight and look at me. I am your Way, your Truth, your Life."

When Jesus heals the deaf, he signals that I can hear new sounds. That I can listen to those speaking to me and not only hear their words, but also interpret what their hearts are saying. There are so many nuances in speech. And when Jesus heals, he gives me a sixth-sense which hears deeper realities.

When he heals the blind, he is giving me a sign that I may be missing a lot of beauty right in front of me.

I may be taking for granted what I see, all the time.

I may be blind or insensitive to the needs I witness daily.

Jesus can open my eyes to see everyday matters with a fresh perspective. To see beauty I have missed and to discern truth with 20/20 vision.

I have only one response. To believe. I really have to believe that Jesus is healing *me*. Trust that Jesus is the healer of *my* hurt, broken, wounded, addicted, accusatory, worrisome, shamed, and unforgiving spirit.

He is the healer of *my* attitudes and actions—even the ones I never knew required healing.

When I look at all the signs Jesus has given me, I realize that maybe being the woman who longs for the ways things could be isn't so far off the mark. Jesus is our healer. Praise God. When we take a step of faith toward the miracle worker in our life, the shaky step of really admitting that we need healing, Jesus does perform miracles.

He does open our ears so we can hear old things in a fresh way.

He does use our meager talents to bless others.

He does calm our storms so we can rest in his security.

He does get rid of our rule boxes filled with "dos" and "don'ts" that, let's face it, don't have as much to do with pleasing God as pleasing those we think might be judging us.

~

In His time, In his time
He makes all things beautiful in his time
Lord, please show me every day
As you're teaching me your way
That you do just what you say
In your time.

—Diane Ball, "In His Time"

~

And at that point, Jesus does reveal a new portion of his amazing grace we never saw before. The portion we need for now. And only the portion we can absorb at the time. Little by little.

And then if we dare to claim the name of Jesus,

allow him to open our eyes,
and clean us,
and help us stand up straight,
and heal us . . .
He frees us.

Step by step. In his time and in his way. He frees us to see and hear and do in love. In his love, the sweetness, fullness, healing, wholeness, peace, clarity, joy, love, acceptance, and kindness we long for are possibilities. Right in our own little corner of the world.

And do you know what? That's a miracle.

He stoops down, touches, and blesses us. And nobody can take that away.

Our fathers can't take that away from us.
Our husbands can't take that away from us.
Our children can't take that away from us.
Our church leaders can't take that away from us.

Our betrayers can't take that away from us.
Our unhealed friends, family, colleagues, and
acquaintances who resent our healing and want us to
stay unhealed can't take that away from us.
No one can take that away from us.

Neither life nor death can separate us from such deep
love.

It cannot go unnoticed how often that kind of healing
takes place in our difficult, painful, and awkward circumstances. Our real internal healing takes place most effectively
in our unhealed moments. Our healing doesn't wait until
every situation in our life is peachy. Until every *i* is dotted
and every *t* is crossed.

And not only does God heal; he prepares meaningful
places for those of us who meet Jesus. To every one of us, he
is able and willing to open our eyes and ears and hearts to
live, serve, and bless others in his kingdom. To every one
of us, he longs to say, "Daughter, go in peace. Your faith has
healed you."

We are women who have met Jesus because Jesus went
out of his way to meet us.

Hallelujah.

The stories in this chapter are found in the following Gospels:
Jesus changes water to wine in John 2:1–11; Jesus heals the man
with leprosy in Mark 1:40–45; Jesus calms the storm in Mark
4:35–41; Jesus drives out an evil spirit in Mark 1:21–28; Jesus
feeds the five thousand in John 6:1–15; Jesus heals the daughter
of the Syrophoenician woman in Mark 7:24–30; Jesus heals
the woman bent over on the Sabbath in Matthew 15:21–28
and Luke 13:10–17;Jesus heals a deaf man in Mark 7:31–37;
and Jesus heals a blind man in Mark 8:22–26.

Process and Dig Deeper

1. What do you long for?

2. Why do you think Jesus desires us to be whole and healed in his kingdom here on earth? What difference does that make in the influence of Christians as they live their lives in this kingdom? After hearing about many of the miracles Jesus performed, what do you think was his primary goal: the actual miraculous sign or the meaning of it for kingdom living?

3. Put yourself in the story of Jesus turning the ceremonial water to wine and ponder: Can you name a person in your life who does not make you feel like you have to live up to a list of "dos" and "don'ts" in order to be a better person? Does someone who accepts you just the way you are readily come to mind? How does it feel to be in the presence of that person? What do you think is the significance for you of Jesus turning the water to wine?

4. Put yourself in the story of Jesus healing the leper, and ponder: Can you name a sin, action, or attitude that you're completely healed of, just as the leper was healed from leprosy? Or do you think that on this side of heaven we are never completely healed of anything? What do you think is the significance for you of Jesus healing the leper?

5. Put yourself in the story of Jesus calming the storm, and ponder: Can you name a recent storm Jesus has calmed in your life? What do you think is the significance for you of Jesus calming the storm?

6. Put yourself in the story of Jesus driving out the evil spirit, and ponder: What persistent bad attitude has Jesus given you power to conquer in your life? To what in your life would you like to say, "Get thee behind me Satan"? What do you think is the significance for you of Jesus telling the evil spirit to "Be Quiet!"?

7. Put yourself in the story of Jesus feeding the masses with a boy's small gift, and ponder: Describe a time when you felt you were doing something out of the "meager" gifts God has given you. How did you bless others by doing that? Did you feel blessed/honored by Jesus? What do you think is the significance for you of Jesus feeding the five thousand with the boy's gift?

8. Put yourself in the story of Jesus healing the daughter of the Syrophoenician woman, and ponder: When Jesus says, "for it is not right to take the children's bread and toss it to their dogs," he is really saying, "toss it to their lap dogs." He was telling her he valued her and was hearing her request while others considered her an intrusion. Have you ever felt protected and shielded by Jesus or by a caring leader? What do you think is the significance for you of Jesus breaking barriers by healing this woman's daughter?

9. Put yourself in the story of the lady bent over and ponder: Are there any legalistic rules from your childhood that you have come to see as rules established for the comfort of the community—having nothing to do with your place before God? What do you think is the significance for you of Jesus helping the woman stand up straight?

10. Put yourself in the stories of the deaf and blind receiving hearing and sight. Ponder: what big and small things do you see

and hear more clearly now than before you knew the healing power of Jesus in your life? What do you think is the significance for you of Jesus healing the deaf and blind?

11. Are you a woman who has met Jesus? Have you met him through these stories of the women in the Gospels? When you think of yourself as a woman who has met Jesus and experienced the grace he offers, what are the results in your life?

12. If you have your own story to share of Jesus' healing, enjoy living that story and blessing others with the grace you have received. If you'd like to share your story with me, email me at ruthvanderzee@gmail.com. When Jesus' story meets our story, beautiful things continue to happen in our lives.

About Ruth Vander Zee

Ruth grew up in a small town on the south side of Chicago. When she married her husband, Vern, she had never been west of the Mississippi River and felt uncomfortable driving more than two hundred miles a day on her honeymoon.

Since then she has lived in four major cities in the United States (from coast to coast) and has travelled extensively throughout the world.

She is a self-described late bloomer, getting her college degree when she was forty, writing her first children's book when she was fifty, and in all the years before and after, raised her three children, played the piano, directed countless musicals, taught middle school, and led many Bible studies.

As the wife of her pastor husband, Vern, she has welcomed thousands of people into her home.

More recently, she has been on the board of Sustaining Pastoral Excellence, planning events and retreats for pastors' spouses.

She presently travels, leading women's retreats and conferences and also visiting schools, talking with students about her books and the writing process.

Her three children are grown and married, and she has four granddaughters.

Ruth is the author of the following books:
Discover Your Gifts And Learn How To Use Them (Faith Alive)
Erika's Story (Creative Editions)
Mississippi Morning, Eli Remembers, and *Always With You* (all published by Eerdmans Books for Young Readers)

Visit Ruth's website: www.journey-of-faith.com